*Working Well at Home*

*By the same author:*

*Life Without Work*
*Panic Attacks*
*101 Ways to Start your Own Business* (Kogan Page)

# Working Well at Home

Coping with the psychological ups and downs
of working where you live

## CHRISTINE INGHAM

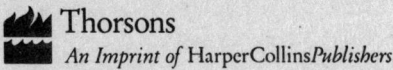
Thorsons
*An Imprint of* HarperCollins*Publishers*

Thorsons
An Imprint of HarperCollins*Publishers*
77–85 Fulham Palace Road,
Hammersmith, London W6 8JB
1160 Battery Street,
San Francisco, California 94111–1213

Published by Thorsons 1995

10 9 8 7 6 5 4 3 2 1

© Christine Ingham 1995

Christine Ingham asserts the moral right to
be identified as the author of this work

A catalogue record for this book
is available from the British Library

ISBN 0 7225 3035 8

Printed in Great Britain by
HarperCollins Manufacturing, Glasgow

# ▪ Contents

# ▪ *Acknowledgements*

I would like to acknowledge the help of: The Henley Centre, the Department of Employment, Home Run, and all those other organizations and individuals who lent their assistance. A special thanks goes to all those who shared with me their own very personal experiences of working at home. This book would have been less than complete without them.

# ▪ *Introduction*

For some years now I've worked from home, originally part-time and now full-time. Like most others who travel along this particular route into self-employment I've encountered difficulties along the way, both practical and personal. The practical issues have been relatively easy to sort out, but the personal ones are where most start to flounder. It is with the aim of addressing these issues that this book has been written.

People can be forgiven for assuming that because these problems are less directly business-related that they are therefore less important, yet personal and interpersonal problems can affect the ultimate success or failure of any business being run from home just as surely as the quality of the product or service being offered. No matter how good a marketing plan or other business strategy you have, if you find yourself suffering from problems with isolation or unsupportive partners, putting those plans into action with any conviction will be that much harder. Unresolved difficulties can easily become a barrier to getting the most out of yourself and therefore your business, too.

There are a whole range of personal challenges waiting for each and every one of us who work at home, whether as free-lancers, teleworkers or entrepreneurs. Learning how to meet those challenges positively is perhaps the greatest of all, because it is only by doing so that we grow as people on both the personal and professional level. Working from home provides us with the ideal opportunity to learn about ourselves as well as simply how to run a business.

Motivation, loneliness, overworking and health are just some of the issues which are tackled, drawing on other people's experiences as well as my own. And although the book is aimed primarily at people who work for themselves, the range of issues covered may be encountered by anyone who works from home, whether employed or self-employed.

It is a practical book with lots of suggestions about how to start developing your own personal strategies for dealing with your individual situation, and hopefully it will enable you to avoid many of the pitfalls which others have encountered. Through this process I also hope you will gradually come to transform your business practice into one which is supportive and actively helps you progress more easily towards a successful future for both your business and yourself.

# 1 ■ *Who Does It?*

**B**irds do it. Bees do it. Perhaps even educated fleas do it. Certainly more and more people are starting to work from home. You may already be one of them, or you may just be at the point of considering whether working from home is for you. Whichever, there is a large body of other home-based workers already established and figures show that it appears to be one area which is rapidly growing. How big is it, though? How many others like yourself are working away in their spare room or even shed? What is the size of this group of workers you might decide to join? Are we talking about a minority of just a few thousand people scattered around the country, or is there a significant number of other homeworkers?

## ■ STATISTICS

The figures quoted for the number of people working from home appear to vary, sometimes quite widely. This may be due to the way in which people themselves classify their activities. Among those who consider themselves to be working from home can be:

- self-employed people who spend the majority of their time working at home
- self-employed people who also use their home as a base but whose work involves them in spending significant periods of the working day elsewhere

- people who are partly self-employed working at home and who also have a job outside the home
- people who are employed but who work at home, including teleworkers
- people who are also employed but who work from their home, using it mainly as a base.

In 1993, the UK's Department of Employment stated that in Great Britain there were '622,000 who stated that they worked in their own home, with 113,000 working for an outside organization'. However, they went on to say that a further '1.33 million worked in a different place but used their home as a base'. Combining these figures we see that almost two million people are, at the latest count, working either at or from home – almost 10 per cent of the workforce. This closely corresponds with the UK magazine *Home Business*'s own estimate of one and a half million, a figure which includes those who are perhaps not necessarily working at home all the time in a purely self-employed capacity.

Research from the Henley Centre shows a definite rise in the number of people working from home, and believes this is closely linked to the sharp increase in the self-employed sector. According to BT's statistics there are now an estimated four million people in Britain who are self-employed; a doubling since 1979. Henley's survey in 1992 showed that, of these, over 40 per cent work from home for some of the time, with 12 per cent working from home all of the time.

In the United States the figures are much higher, with a staggering 41 million people in 1993 working at home – a third of the total adult workforce. More than half of these are self-employed: 24.3 million, or almost 20 per cent of the work force; twice the figure of the UK.

If the enterprise culture continues to grow in the UK, we may find similar figures being reached, perhaps in the not-too-distant future. Advances in technology are making it easier for business, professional and also creative people to take the opportunity of becoming self-employed. The advent of more powerful personal computers, the growth in professional software packages, affordable facsimile machines appearing on the market, advances in telecommunications to allow computers to 'talk' to each other remotely, as well as the development of down-sized versions of basic office equipment such as photocopiers, all now make the possibility of working independently at home a very real prospect for many people.

So, although people working from home are in the minority compared with the total workforce, it is definitely a considerably significant minority. Yet who makes up these numbers? Are they still women from lower down the economic scale working for 'pin' money? Or is the picture somewhat different?

The answer is both 'yes' and 'no'. Women make up about two thirds of those who work from home, so they are still in the majority there. However, the work they do is very different from what they may have been associated with in the past. Figures from the Department of Employment on employees who work at home show that although the traditionally female areas of secretarial, word-processing and administrative work are, nine times out of ten, done by women, three out of four writers and journalists are women; two out of three training and education workers are female; and approximately half of managers, sales staff, marketing and research workers are women, too. Perhaps surprisingly, they also form a very large minority – 48 per cent – in the traditionally male area of engineering. Men, however, are in the majority in other fields: 84 per cent of consultants, 86 per cent of computer professionals and 96 per cent of accountants and others in the financial services industry. Interestingly, men also form the majority of those who work from home as a base.

Although men and women have shows of strength in different fields, there are obviously representations across the board of both sexes in all areas. This is a very different picture from the commonly held view of people who work from home, no doubt based on the history of homeworking.

## ■ A BRIEF HISTORY OF HOMEWORKING

Glancing back through the annals of time and civilization's history we find at its beginning the original homeworkers. Survival in its most raw sense was the name of the game. First there were the cave-dwellers who lived by hunting and gathering their food. Then once land cultivation was learned, the foragers and wanderers began to settle down to a home base around which their daily existence revolved. Both men's and women's work was dictated by the demands of the home, although women tended to stay nearer the home base particularly if they had children, while the men tended to work further away from the home base, going out on foraging or hunting trips for the family's food or to tend the land. It seems that little has changed in that women, at present, still form the greater number of those who work at home, while there are greater numbers of men who use the home as a base from which to work.

With the advent of the industrial revolution both men and women in the working classes began to reverse the established pattern and started to leave the home to work in thriving factories. Families in the higher classes maintained servants to carry the burden of much of the work around the house. Home-work became relegated to the preserve of women who might take in washing or, for the more genteel, become seam-stresses. The work was generally poorly paid.

Gradually, through this century, women became more tied to the house as housewives, apart from during the war years when they performed many of the jobs outside the home which had previously been considered 'man's work'. However, the return to the home this time was a far cry from the pre-industrial days when both men and women had equal, if different, work interests in and around the home. Now, in poorer families where the woman was tied to the house while she had children, she sometimes turned to poorly paid, home-based piece work to help supplement the family's income. Further up the social scale, housework became synonymous with drudgery, boredom and sometimes social isolation; men, on the other hand, continued to work away from home. The pendulum was ripe to swing again.

Eventually women became disgruntled with their unde-manding existence, while others who were influenced by the sexual liberation of the 1960s set their sights on something other than settling down into domesticity. And so we saw the rise of The Career Woman. Men were still, in the main, working away from home chasing their own careers. They were also still coming home with the expectation that their wife or partner was going to maintain all the housework and child-rearing duties as well as her new career.

For many women this 'double whammy' proved unworkable – understandably. However, the change in family economies meant that two incomes were no longer just desirable but a necessity.

Now throw into the mixture the growth in the enterprise culture which began in the 1980s. Add a large portion of redundancies and the prospect of dwindling job pools. Stir in with huge cost-cutting measures taken by businesses to cut over-heads by harnessing the power of modern technology and employing people to do their job of work from their own homes. Combine with growing dissatisfaction with the personal cost and expense of sometimes having to commute vast distances daily to work. Now leave to prove. Hey presto! We have a rising home-based work culture.

It seems that the pendulum is moving back closer to its start position. The home is again being seen as something other than that which we come back to after eight to ten hours' absence. For a large number of people it is again becoming the place around which their lives can revolve, rather than something which they move to and from, so that it has become almost an appendage to their working lives; but more of that later.

Both men and women are again seeing benefits to working at home – but what types of people are deciding to adopt this style of working, and what sorts of businesses or freelance activities are they involved in? Are self-employed home-based workers now all high-flying professionals of the thirty-something brigade, playing business games on their lap-tops, or is the field somewhat wider?

## ■ TYPES OF PEOPLE

For some people, working from home can open doors to many opportunities which would otherwise remain firmly closed to them.

### People with Children

Those who wish to combine a career with child-rearing may have experienced difficulties in the regular job market. Working from home provides the flexibility to be with your children while still developing your career and generating an income.

Since women are most often associated with child-rearing this may be the reason why there are more women than men who work solely or primarily at home rather than using it as more of a base. However, this is not always the case. Simon for instance, found that by working from home he could have a greater share in bringing up his children than if he were out 'at the office' for most of the day. When he started working from home his daughter Jo was three years old and his son Aran had been born just six months earlier. 'I enjoyed being more involved with the children. And later, when they were older I used to take Jo to school in the morning and pick her up at the end of the day. I could structure my day around it, and it gave me a basic framework to the day.'

## Single Parents

For single parents especially, working from home may solve a lot of otherwise difficult problems. Dounne Alexander-Moore, who established her business 'Gramma's' (which makes herbal pepper sauces), became *Options* magazine's best newcomer in the 'Women Mean Business' awards sponsored by TSB Unit Trusts. It was after leaving her husband and taking her two teenage daughters with her to set up home afresh that she turned to the idea of working for herself to improve her difficult financial situation. Working at home may provide single parents with the opportunity to juggle the practical and financial demands of bringing up a family on your own.

## Carers

There may also be other types of family commitments which make the home the most appropriate place to work. Looking after family members who may have a long-term illness or disability can mean that working outside the home becomes very difficult, if not impossible. Providing that the care element is not a full-time occupation in itself, becoming self-employed and working from home can be a way of being able to accommodate this sort of commitment while enabling the carer to pursue and develop his or her own interests and career.

As the ageing population increases, more people may be starting to approach the prospect of making at-home provision for their parents or other older relatives who, while not necessarily ill, may benefit from having close supervision, contact or simply companionship. This could be an expensive provision to 'buy in', but something which could fit in with the caring relative's own work at home.

## Retired People

The ageing population also provides another category of home-workers: people who have retired. Of the people who have contributed to this book with their own personal experiences of being self-employed and working from home, two were retired: Gerald, who had been an accountant and has now turned his skills and experience to his advantage through consultancy work, and Richard, who had previously held a high-ranking position in the Foreign Service and who decided after his retirement to investigate the possibilities within the field of writing. Like Gerald, he also became involved in consultancy work, using the valuable experience he had gained during the many years in his previous work.

Many who have reached retirement age may also come to investigate the possibilities which working for themselves from home might offer.

## People with Disabilities

Another contribution to my research came from Lara, who became disabled through ill-health but did not qualify for any benefits. Working from home provided her with the answer to how she could work within her limits while generating an income for herself. She set herself up in business maintaining graves for people who were unable to do so themselves.

Although many employers are becoming more educated about and familiar with taking on people with disabilities, there is still a lot of silent discrimination which takes place and militates against succeeding with job applications. Breaking through this barrier can be incredibly difficult. Finding an employer who hires people based on their abilities and who provides the opportunity to utilize and develop those skills is not an easy task. If you have a disability and can't find that almost mythical creature – an exemplary employer – deciding to become that person yourself can enable you to circumvent those issues and provide the answer to what might seem to be an insurmountable problem. Working at home for yourself means you can tailor your work to suit your own abilities and provide a means to develop them to the full.

## Newly Self-employed

Many people who make the decision to start their own business do so on a self-employed basis, and many of these decide to work from home, at least in the initial stages. In the next chapter we will have a look in more detail at some of the reasons why people choose to make that decision. But besides those who work at home only during the initial phase of self-employment, there are also those for whom their home will always be the place where they carry out their business activities.

Working from home appears to cross all boundaries, regardless of age, sex, disability, or even paper qualifications. There are people with MBAs or other letters after their names, but there are equally those with not much more than a straightforward, basic education. In this respect it seems that there is no special 'type' of person who works at home, although doing so may provide a neat solution and wonderful opportunity for certain groups of people.

But what sort of activities are they engaged in? What sort of work lends itself to being carried out in the home environment? Does it always involve a computer and the use of high technology, or are other types of businesses being successfully run from home?

## ▪ TYPES OF BUSINESS

Even within the relatively small sample of people with whom I made contact, a surprisingly wide range of business activities was revealed. They, and others, illustrate the diversity of home businesses which are successfully being run by an equally diverse range of individuals.

Home businesses may be grouped into the following categories:

### Telework

This generally refers to work which is carried out by employees in their own home, involving the use of information technology. However, there are opportunities for self-employed people in this area, too. The sorts of jobs which fit into this category are: keyboard operating, data input, software engineering and computer programming.

## Freelance Work

Many professions are open to freelance work. Working very much as an individual, in the majority of cases the home is the most sensible place to work or use as a base.

Carol operates in this way in her work as a journalist. Similarly, Hal works from home in his chosen field as a freelance researcher for film and video production companies.

Editors, proof-readers, indexers, translators, copywriters as well as photographers can all be found among the people who classify themselves as freelance workers.

## Production and Manufacturing

Whether it's making hot pepper sauces like Dounne Alexander-Moore, baking bread or making gifts, the home can provide the base from which to work. It might be less than ideal if what you are making demands lots of space or special conditions, and regulations do exist concerning manufacturing businesses in a residential setting, so there may be limitations on what you can and can't do. On the other hand, if you are producing something like a publication your home might be an ideal place to work.

Alice works at home producing crafts which she then sells through retail outlets and at craft fairs. She doesn't use any heavy equipment or handle noxious substances so the special regulations don't apply to her. Working from home is her best option at present.

## Consultancy Work

Consultancy work can provide an ideal solution for the person who has gained good experience in a particular field of work while in employment and who becomes interested in the self-employed option.

Consultants market and sell their experience and knowledge. They advise others on the best course of action to take to remedy a situation or problem area, basing their decision on their knowledge, experience and any assessments they might carry out.

PR, marketing, training and finance are all areas which lend themselves to consultancy work, but so too are the arts-based fields such as design and antiques.

Operating this type of business from home seems to be an obvious step to take. You need little more than basic office equipment to get going, and most meetings are held at the client's own business premises. Paying for costly office space would seem to be an unnecessary expense, especially in the early days or if you are certain you wish to remain small, operating as a sole trader with no plans for expansion.

## Agencies

As with consultancy work, there are few requirements to setting up an agency. A telephone, filing cabinet and desk are the main ones, and these can fit easily into your home space.

Agencies serve as go-betweens. You may be an estate agent, baby-sitting agent or employment agent. The now famous Brook Street Bureau secretarial agency started out as a home-based business. Marjorie Hurst went into business from her flat in Portsmouth after her husband left her with two small children. She's now a millionaire.

## Business Services

Accountants, architects, market researchers, surveyors, typists and trainers – these can all loosely be grouped under the heading Business Services, although some are more strictly professional/technical occupations. However, they do all serve or support other businesses to a greater or lesser degree and they can all operate from home.

In most cases meetings will be held at the client's own business premises, so expensive rented office accommodation can be an unnecessary overhead if you already have adequate space at home in which to work.

Derek provides financial services from his home in Yorkshire. Meetings take place in either the client's home or office space. Similarly, Hilary's work as a trainer and training consultant takes her into her client's place of work for briefings and to carry out the training sessions and courses. She only needs basic office space in which to prepare her work, and this is provided by her small spare room which she has converted into her at-home office.

## Arts

Some artists prefer to have a dedicated studio space in which to work where the amount of mess they make is of no consequence. This space may be available within the home.

Apart from fine artists, there are others working in the arts field who also work from home – such as cartoonists, interior designers, writers and video producers.

Liz is a graphic designer and chose to work from her home in the beautiful Buckinghamshire countryside when she decided to become self-employed. And for Barry, an author living in London, working from home seemed the most sensible option, as it is for most writers.

## Service Sector

Many self-employed and small businesses are in the service sector – offering and providing a particular service to businesses, homes or individuals. The group is diverse, including complementary health practitioners, counselling services, maintenance work such as gardening or plumbing, and clerical services like typing and telephone answering services.

In some instances the service is provided in the client's own home or office. In others the client visits the practitioner's own home, as is the case with David, a complementary health therapist working in Somerset. His patients travel miles to receive treatment, which is carried out in a therapy room in his family home which he has set aside specially for the purpose.

For Lara, her home provided the base from which to work, running her business looking after graves for surviving friends and relatives. Arrangements with clients are normally carried out by letter and phone, which could easily be managed from her home, as is the case with many service sector businesses.

So, to return to the question 'Who Does It?', we can see that:

- A growing number of people are starting to work from home.
- A wide range of different types of people from all sorts of backgrounds are doing it.
- Both men and women are now homeworkers.
- People are running a very diverse range of businesses.

Working at or from home now appears to be cutting across all boundaries. It is on the increase and, because of other influences (for example, continued down-sizing of large companies), it may continue to do so for some time. Whether you are already established as a homeworker or are simply contemplating the move, you may rest assured that there are many hundreds of thousands also doing the same. But the next question is, why and how do people decide to work from home?

# 2 ▪ Why Work from Home?

The only constant in life is change. What may have once appeared to be a secure and stable future with its own sure-footed tread can suddenly be altered by wayward external forces with what seems like hardly a moment's notice. On the other hand, change can come about gradually and from within; it can take you by surprise to find that the hidden enemy is in fact none other than yourself and your own drives and dreams. Either way, when change affects your working life new options become open to investigation, and working from home in a self-employed capacity may be one of them.

Perhaps there are as many different reasons for deciding to work at home as there are homeworkers. But it may be useful to have a look at some of those reasons and the way in which people have reached the decision to steer their working life in this new, alternative direction. Having a look at the decision-making process from other people's perspectives may help to clarify your own objectives and reasons for doing what you are doing, or may help you to form a more soundly reasoned argument and understanding as to why you might take your next career step along this particular path.

Being clear about why you are doing what you are doing is important. It enables you to develop appropriate coping strategies; it gives you a basis from which you can define, mould and refine your vision for your working future and how you would like things to be; and it can also provide a greater sense of security about your own personal journey which has brought you to this point and which is about to carry you forward.

So let's look at a few of the many factors that may influence your decision to work from home.

## ▪ THE WORLD OF WORK

### Employment Fall-out

Over recent years the effects of the recession and the impact of new technology have been felt by all. A sense of insecurity about our employment and personal economic futures has crept into our lives and embraced each of us. The firing guns may have been sounded in your area, and even if you were some way distant you will have heard the dreaded rumblings signal the alert to you, too. The effect has been felt throughout the workforce in all but some of the Far Eastern countries, although even Japan is starting to feel the shock waves now.

### Redundancy

One direct effect of the recession has been that companies have gone under, sometimes leaving masses of floundering redundant workers in their wake. Lifelines have been few, with the knock-on effects rippling through other related sectors of the economy, capsizing other businesses in turn. Redundancy, as if that weren't hard enough to bear, can often be followed by a long period of unemployment. The combination of scant vacancies and few, if any, suitable opportunities has left many feeling only bleakness and despair. Many decide to take the reins in their own hands and steer a course into self-employment – like Hal, who was made redundant at the beginning of the 1990s. He was in his mid-forties when, like many others, he lost his middle-management position within London's education authority when it was disbanded:

> *I looked for jobs but nothing which interested me was avail-able or achievable, or I was over-qualified, so I had to think of other ways of earning money. I had to look at ways of using skills which I'd already acquired – this led me into research work. I became a freelance researcher. Before settling into this I also did lots of odd-jobbing work which I thoroughly enjoyed.*

Hal had no great entrepreneurial dream; it wasn't that which took him into working for himself at home. Neither was this the case for Alice with her crafts-based business, who admits, 'I couldn't get work, and was encouraged to set up in business on my own under the Government Allowance Scheme.' As for many others, working from home simply emerged as the only viable alternative in a difficult, if not hostile, job market.

## Promotion Problems

Even companies managing to survive the economic doldrums may be doing so only at the cost of carrying out massive restruc-turing exercises to down-size their business, perhaps by flattening out of existence some of the various management levels.

The effect of such measures, for those not actually made redundant, is that promotion prospects diminish. And since the same is occurring in other businesses, even sideways (let alone promotional) moves to other companies have also become more difficult. Under these circumstances the decision to go freelance and work from home was the inevitable solution for Carol, who '…was not getting the appointments which I was applying for, so I decided to go freelance as a reporter/researcher'.

## Job Dissatisfaction

Being passed over for promotion, limited job prospects, an insecure future, selling a product that isn't wanted – any of the myriad frustrations that can befall someone in employment can culminate in strong feelings of job dissatisfaction, bringing with it undue levels of stress. As Hilary, a single thirty-something in London says, 'I was not enjoying what I was doing. Also I was about to be made redundant. I thought if I worked as a freelance trainer I would have less stress.' Similarly Gilly, who had previously been working in education, decided to opt for working for herself, initially from home, importing artefacts from the Far East. She decided she wanted to 'escape and avoid the frustrations previously experienced' which she says resulted for her in feelings of 'diminished individuality'.

## Casualized Workforce

Another outcome of the pressures facing businesses has been the casualization of the workforce. Instead of recruiting people on a permanent basis, work is farmed out where possible to freelancers, temporary staff or key-time workers who are retained and called in during peak periods. Wherever possible, employers are now subcontracting on a competitive tendering basis – which means that work goes to people outside the firm or organization.

This has obviously meant redundancy for some, and for those who remain behind a deepening sense of insecurity. Those who have been keeping their eye on the ball and have seen it bouncing in the direction it has, may have decided to play it to their advantage and become one of the freelancers for whom their previous employer can now provide work.

## Retirement

Many look forward to the day when they can legitimately put an end to the nine-to-five. However, for others this is not necessarily the case, as with Richard: 'On retiring I wanted to find another job or jobs, so set myself up on a self-employed basis.' He worked from his flat in London, writing and carrying out consultancy work. The same applied to Gerald: 'Having retired from British Telecom, I did not wish to give up work altogether.'

Exploring the self-employment possibilities on retirement is one way of maintaining an active, if less demanding, work schedule which can effectively be run from your own home.

Given the continuing difficulties in the job market brought about by the recession, changes in employment practices, and sometimes because of political decisions, many people appear to gravitate towards self-employment from home as a coping strategy. 'I had no real desire [to work from home],' says Simon, a 43-year-old management consultant, 'but chose it because of a lack of suitable jobs and because I also thought the experience would be good.'

For some it would seem that the decision to become self-employed has been initially prompted less by an inner entrepreneurial driving force and perhaps more by a quiet desperation. As a result of individual circumstances, starting out has, for them, inevitably meant starting from home. Your own reasons for deciding to work for yourself may be similar or quite different from these. The point is, if it seems the most appropriate course of action, take it; certainly it is one way of, at the very least, seeing yourself through to the next stage of your career and working life.

## ▪ PERSONAL AND HOME CIRCUMSTANCES

### Family Commitments

Juggling the demands of a young family and of having a job outside the home can be very difficult. Yet staying at home with a two-year-old, bantering in words of no more than one syllable, can be stultifying. If you want to stay at home with your children, yet still want to make use of and develop your abilities, running a business from home might be the answer. This applies equally to those who are looking after their children and to those caring for elderly relatives or others in the home who rely on your presence. It solves the problem of feeling that you are missing out by no longer being in the job market.

### Being Housebound

Compounding the problem of job shortages, your geographical location may make working outside the home even more difficult. The nearest job market may be too distant and transport links too infrequent. Without having transport of your own, finding a suitable job can end up disappearing into the realms of improbability. However, this has been the spur which has goaded some into considering setting up an enterprise at home. Many opportunities exist which suit the housebound or people living in remote areas. Mail order businesses, for example, and telework (using computers in conjunction with telecommunication's new technology) are not dependent on being near the markets or clients they might be serving. In this case it doesn't matter if you live in an unemployment black-spot with the nearest source of employment some 60 or 100 miles away and only one bus service between them. Running your own business from home enables you to side-step these otherwise insurmountable problems.

## Disability

Although it shouldn't do, having a disability can prove to be another hurdle placed slap in the middle of your career path. You may or may not be housebound, but if finding a suitable job which has the sort of challenges you are looking for is proving more than just a little difficult, then generating your own work may be your way forward. As Lara says, 'It was pride more than anything' which led her to set up her grave-maintenance business. 'I was on Sickness Benefit and then an assessment doctor decided I was "not ill enough" to carry on receiving the benefit. He said I should get a job. I felt very ill at the time and in fact, a year later I was in hospital with severe artery trouble. But in the meantime I just thought "What the hell am I going to do?" I got drunk one night and the thought about the business just came to me. It has been a great job. I borrowed my mum's car to help me out and it took off beautifully.'

Employers may see only the disability when you apply for a job. Working for yourself from home enables you to ignore such attitudes and work with what you know are your strengths and abilities.

## Money

Without doubt, money is the one thing which all of the respondents I consulted when starting to write this book referred to. Money, as they say, makes the world go round; and it is certainly the point around which the decision to work from home centres for many people.

## A Second Income

The financial demands of family life mean that a second income is becoming less of a welcome additional boost and more of a necessity. Even without that necessity, being aware of the fragile state of the employment market can prove to be the motivating factor behind wanting to develop another string to the family's financial bow. Starting small with an enterprise which can be run from the back bedroom can be a convenient way in which to start generating an income which is not dependent upon the vagaries of the job market and disinclined bosses.

## The Start-up Syndrome

Starting any new business costs money, and if you haven't enough of it the business may fail as a result. Under-funding is one of the main reasons behind business failure. It makes sense, then, that the fewer overheads a new venture has, the more easily it can improve its prospects.

Many of the people I interviewed for this book felt that office accommodation was one area where they could make a significant saving. By using their home as an office instead of paying out additional (and sometimes quite heavy) rental costs for business premises they could instantly produce a positive effect on their cashflow. As Simon says, 'I could see no reason to pay high rents every week for an office. The money may as well go into my business.'

Logistically, deciding to run a business from home when starting up may be the most sensible way to operate in the early days. Even without financial pressures, working from home makes sense until you can see how the business is going to develop and what its future space and location needs are likely to be. And should the venture prove to be an almighty flop, at least if you are working from home you will not have the problem of trying to get out of leases or incur the costs of vacating office premises.

### Rental Costs

You may ideally see your business operating from a prime site with you rubbing commercial shoulders with 'Big Boys Plc'. Reality may take a different form.

Derek, who is self-employed in the financial services industry, considered operating from retail premises. However, on doing some basic research he quickly realized that 'High Street shop rentals were too high.' His initial plans were foiled, but now he is happily working from home and saving the money he would otherwise be spending on premises. Especially in the early days, finding money to pay for the ideal working environment may be something which just has to wait until the business has established itself and the additional finance for rent can more easily be included in the budget.

For others, the decision to work at home may have come about as a result of having to relocate after having become established in retail, commercial or other business premises. With sharp increases in business rates, the once viable operation can easily start to flounder; add on rent rises and soon it can become only too clear that changes need to be made. If the increases cannot be passed on to clients and customers, and other budgetary economies fail to make up for the new financial demands, then finding new premises from which to operate may become the next most obvious step to consider. For some this step may be to relocate to your own home base.

## Type of Business

The decision to work from home may be a relatively simple one for people running particular types of business. Although

William, who works as a freelance radio producer, has to deliver the end product in a recording studio, that is only one part (although obviously an important one) of the total amount of work he does. 'All the preparation takes place at a desk and on the phone – working from home was the logical thing to do.'

This appears to be many people's reasoning, especially when their work involves going to or carrying out work at clients' premises. Operating from separate business premises creates a travel triangle: home, office, clients' premises. Working from home eliminates one of the travel points, saving time and expense.

Similarly, some occupations are best entered through the self-employment route. David, a complementary health practitioner, explains the simple reason why he chose to become self-employed: 'The work I do, natural healing, is hard to find employment in with any organization. Self-employment was really the only practical way.'

The sort of work you do or want to do, and how you operate, can thus be critical factors in your decision that self-employment is the best way forward and that working from home is the natural, sometimes only feasible choice.

## Personal Evolution

Self-employment may be a dream which is assiduously worked towards, a goal whose attainment is very much the focus of a person's life. A desire to join the ranks of entrepreneurs leads some people resolutely forward, never really happy until they are running their own show.

For others, becoming self-employed appears to be something which evolves out of their present lifestyle or activities rather than as the result of some burning ambition. The development of hobbies or other leisure pursuits is a common way in which this sort of evolution can take place. You may come to realize gradually that besides enjoying doing what you do and receiving praise from others, people will also willingly pay for the proceeds of your hobby. Whether you have a real flair for making homemade chocolates, cakes or bread, or a comprehensive knowledge of fly-fishing, you may come to feel that since you have the competence and have more than completed your apprenticeship, you may as well charge people for receiving the benefits of your skills and knowledge. A grand launch befitting a new business is not so much the case here as a quiet continuation of what you have been doing – with the important difference that from Monday you will begin to receive an income for your efforts.

Even without a hobby or pastime easing you into self-employment, circumstances and opportunities can arise, grab hold of your imagination's hand and lead you towards the realization that you really could make a go of it. Under these circumstances you might find yourself with more of a 'Let's have a go' attitude.

I knew Charles when he was head of department, teaching in a secondary school. If you'd asked me then, I would have said that he was set for life in the education world. To some extent I would have been right, but his life has led him away from employment in the state sector and into self-employment in his own home. Charles decided that he wanted a break from mainstream teaching and initially decided to work on a temporary basis for a private college. In the meantime he met and married his Hungarian wife. Charles explains:

*She has a teaching degree in English and Hungarian, and we wished to use her qualifications. We soon found, after an initial period of part-time Hungarian teaching, that there was 1) a gap in the market – no one else was doing it well; and*

*2) a favourable climate after 1989 with the opening up of Eastern Europe. The Hungarian government was the most active of all Eastern European governments in attracting Western investment, therefore more Hungarian translations and tuition were required.*

Charles identified the gap, perceived the need and found himself responding to it. This once-staid teacher is now a very successful entrepreneur. The opportunity presented itself and the shift from local government employee to self-employed entrepreneur became an almost seamless transition.

Sometimes opportunities do present themselves in this way – take the case Simon who began his consultancy work some 10 years ago. When asked what his reasons were for going into self-employment, he states matter-of-factly, 'Opportunity. I was asked to carry out some lucrative contracts.' No great business plan to follow or toiling away at marketing strategies beforehand. The move into consultancy work for him was again more a case of being in the right place at the right time to seize the opportunity as it arose, taking him into the world of self-employment and running his own business.

## Personality

Our own personal drives and needs can also play a large part in determining a move towards self-employment. Although Simon was presented with an opportunity to work for himself, reaching the decision to do so was subconsciously influenced by the type of person he is. He describes himself as a loner who doesn't like having to mix with people. He sees himself as shy and reserved, and says he can find it difficult to make contact with others. With these personality traits, being in employment and having to work alongside other colleagues can become difficult and stressful. For him, working on his own has enabled him to avoid these stresses.

Gilly was also similarly spurred on towards self-employment through wanting to 'escape and avoid the frustrations previously experienced'.

I believe that finding a job which suits our personalities is just as important as finding one which uses our skills. For some people, being able to work in and around the home with only minimal business contact with others may prove to be the most appropriate and satisfactory way in which to work.

## Work Cultures

The type of work colleagues you encounter in employment can also influence your decision to want to go solo. This compounded the uncomfortable work situation for Simon, whose workmates he described as yuppies whom he perceived as having no connection with what he saw as real life. Certainly, having to work alongside these sorts of people left him with the feeling that it wasn't where he was at, or wanted to be. If you don't feel as though you fit in, the obvious reaction is to want to get out.

Not fitting in with the traditional work culture may manifest itself through sensing a definite desire for autonomy. Gilly realized she wanted 'independence, action and some real control'. She also realized she was unlikely to get what she wanted by staying put in her job. At a dinner party one evening while a conversation about difficulties at work rolled on around her, she suddenly decided – and announced – that she was going to resign when she went back to work on Monday. And she did.

Like others, myself included, Gilly wanted to have some control over both day-to-day events and her own destiny. Shrugging off the shackles imposed by managers and company cultures allows you the freedom to run with your own ideas, test them out and forge your own way ahead without having to answer to others, without having them veto your suggestions or make you fill out forms in triplicate first.

By identifying your own drives and ambitions you may be able to discover why employment will always leave you dissatisfied, regardless of which job you do and in what sort of cultural or physical environment you are expected to work. Analysing your working life in this way can lead you to a better understanding and acceptance that a more positive alternative is a work environment which you create for yourself, albeit at the kitchen table to begin with.

## Physical Environment

For some, the physical environment in which they work is not of paramount importance. However, for others this can be a major deciding factor in where they work. Some occupations require adequate facilities and space, as for mechanics or potters. Other occupations might require fewer facilities and need only a desk or drawing board – but the surrounding environment is just as important and can have its psychological effect on you.

I remember working for one organization which was based in a very grim building. It was located in a remote area in a rundown part of town, overlooking a main intersection of motorways. It was not only poorly decorated, it was also badly maintained – grimy windows, peeling walls, inadequate heating. Despite being enthusiastic about the work I was doing, that particular place of work, which offered little in the way of visual or other comforts, eventually began to affect the way I felt about going to and being in work. Thankfully the business relocated to more modern offices which had better basic facilities and which were adequately decorated and maintained. The psychological shift which occurred as a result was remarkable.

Liz, in her work as a graphic designer, felt very acutely the need for an environment which was more sympathetic to her creative nature. Wanting to 'be in an environment of my own choice and under my control' was for her the main reason for deciding to work from home. 'To be able to walk into the garden and talk to my chickens; to sit and drink tea by the fire' was what she felt she needed in her working life. Addressing those needs meant she could work more effectively and contentedly without having to cope with the distractions and depressing effect of a grubby, uninspiring workplace.

On the other hand, there may be more practical reasons influencing your decision to work from home. Gerald lives with his wife in their family home. His decision to set up his business there was made that much easier because of the available space. 'Fortunately,' he explains 'we have a bedsitter at the top of our house which I am able to use as an office.' Indeed, why pay rent for business premises when space is available closer to home?

## Going Solo

Necessity and the type of operation you are running may also be deciding factors when weighing up whether you should go it alone. For example, as a writer it would make little sense for me personally to bring in a partner, although writing partnerships are not unheard of. Artists tend to work alone, as do most who establish a business which is based on their own existing skills, knowledge or expertise.

If you are providing a second income through your business activities (the main one being brought in by your partner), perhaps combined with raising your family, being a solo worker may be the most obvious way in which to start off your business. This will also be the case if your business is developing out of a hobby or other leisure pursuit.

From the outset Gerald saw his business in a solely self-employed light. 'I had no particular wish to take on a partner,' he says, 'and in any case it is a lot easier to set up as a management consultant on one's own.' Derek held a more jaundiced view of working with others. 'Partnerships hardly ever work,' he claims. Whether you agree with this or not, what is important is that you establish a working set-up which suits your own particular needs and inclinations as well as the dictates of the job itself.

## Lifestyle Goals

Working for yourself may be a way in which you can see how you might attain other personal life goals. The work may not necessarily be the goal itself, but it may provide the means by which you can reach those longed-for and cherished lifestyle or financial aims.

If you want to work only when you need to, running a small enterprise from home may be the way in which you can achieve that particular aim. If you want to spend as much time as possible travelling and seeing the world, you may decide that working from home is the most likely way in which you can do so. The flexibility of being able to down tools – and pick them up again when you come back – may be the best way forward to help you do just exactly that.

Working from home need not be the reason in itself for becoming self-employed; it may provide the means to another, quite different but possibly more important personal end point.

## ▪ WHY DO *YOU* WANT TO WORK FROM HOME?

We've had a look at many reasons why people decide to work from home. They are pretty wide-ranging – from having a nice place to work to finding a personal answer to unemployment. I believe it is important for you to know why you want to set up and run a business from home, and although we'll have a more detailed look at goals later on (Chapter 8) it may be useful here to consider why you want to do so, perhaps before you make any final decisions.

Think about what it is that is driving you towards considering this work option. If it is that you want to escape an impossible boss, would a personal skills course to teach you how to handle difficult people more effectively be the real answer? If you want to escape from an unsatisfactory work situation, would a simple change of job become more possible if you improved your qualifications or your job-seeking and interview skills? You may relish the idea of developing your hobby into a business, but is it really viable, and might the enjoyment you take in it at present diminish when you have to do it day in, day out? A soul's cry for freedom from the nine-to-five might appear to have found its answer in self-employment, working in the cosy confines of home, but be clear about what freedom actually means before deciding that working at home would provide you with it. A pretty place to work might be achieved in your present job by negotiating with your employer for improved conditions. Does the prospect of challenging your boss cause you to cower? Then how will you handle difficult customers when you're working for yourself or negotiating terms with hard-nosed suppliers? Developing your negotiating skills might be the real answer to getting what you want out of your work situation, not scurrying home and trying to close the door on the demands of the world of work.

Having said that, difficult or negative situations can be used to propel you forward in life. But what may prove less satisfactory is viewing working from home as a means of escape, as a bolt-hole for when things become too difficult at work. As we shall see later, homeworking is not necessarily a bed of roses, and self-employment in any form is incredibly hard work in itself.

So take time to analyse why you want to work from home. Clarify your reasons and ensure they form a positive part of your overall business and life plan. It means you need to be clear on the workability of your idea, not only in terms of whether you can make and sell enough widgets to keep the business viable, but also in terms of whether it will be workable as a home-based business. That may be a little more difficult to quantify, but hopefully by reading the rest of this book you will get a clearer picture of any potential areas of difficulty and how you might be able to work around or with them. But before we consider the difficulties, let's look at some of the many advantages to working from home which people have been discovering for themselves, because in order for you to make a balanced decision you need to be aware of *all* the angles – both good and bad.

# 3 ▪ *The Pluses*

As we have seen, there are many reasons why people decide to work from home. Sometimes it is their circumstances and sometimes their own needs and desires which take them in this new direction, hoping that their expectations will be met and needs fulfilled, and aware of the processes which have led them to the decision that this is the next most logical step.

But what about after you have started up? How does the reality compare with the dream? In this chapter we will have a look at some of the pluses; the advantages to be gained which emerge out of the new experience and which may not necessarily have been anticipated beforehand. Indeed, some of the positive elements could not be foreseen because they form part of the dynamics of the evolving situation and come about as a result of your own personal interaction with that process.

Most initial concerns in the early days tend to be centred around practicalities. Any advantages which might have been anticipated are given little time and instead are glossed over in the urgent rush to sort out bookkeeping, marketing and getting that fax machine installed. However, it might be worth your while to find time to give due consideration to them. Without having an awareness of the possible advantages it might be only too easy to concentrate on the difficulties of working at home and to end up with the feeling that you've made a mistake before you've even started.

Being aware of the pluses of any situation is also important. They can provide some welcome additional ammunition which you might need to gun down any opposition to your proposed plans from partners or mutinous family members (more about them in Chapter 9). At the very least, being aware of them can help you make a more balanced appraisal about what to expect; for those already established in their home business it might provide an opportunity to reappraise your own situation and reflect on some of the positive elements which you might be overlooking in the rush to make that next sale. Occasionally reminding yourself about them can be just as important as doing the filing, since these positive factors can help to buoy you up when you find yourself going through the inevitable bad patches.

So let's have a look at some of these positive spin-offs to homeworking.

## ▪ FINANCIAL ADVANTAGES

### Effect of Low Overheads

Wanting to keep overheads low by not having to rent business premises is a common reason for deciding to operate from home. The rental costs are normally the main and often only focus for making that decision, but hidden within that choice lie other advantages.

After you have done your research and declared to the world your intent to work for yourself, one of the first tasks is to establish your work environment. If you were to rent separate premises rather than work from home you would find yourself incurring moving costs: transporting furniture, equipment and other office necessities; installing a telephone; redecorating; providing your own basic catering facilities; your time involved in making the move, and so on. But if you start off working at home, you can often use some available furniture to create your office 'environment', even if it is only the kitchen table to begin with. Later on you might need some special office storage space for stationery and files, but right now you can clear out a drawer or two as your starting point. Similarly, you may find that most of the other office necessities on your list can already be found in or around your home – at no additional cost to you, and incurring minimal time and actual cost to 'move' into your new office. You're already off to a good financial start and reaping one of your first financial benefits.

Another cost which can be overlooked when renting business premises is cleaning. Since the area in which you are going to work at home would be cleaned anyway, regardless of whether it was your office space or not, more savings are made by avoiding this additional expense (unless you want to encourage the entrepreneurial spirit in younger family members and give them your office cleaning contract!)

Service charges are often levied on commercial tenants on top of the rent they are paying. Among other things, the charge usually covers heating and lighting. Sometimes this is worked out according to actual usage, but it is also usual for the charge to be made regardless of how much or how little you use. This obviously takes control of the charges out of your hands and you can end up subsidizing other office users who have full overhead and desk lighting on constantly, and the heating turned up even in summer. With your business based at home you can exercise total control over these expenses, which may certainly lead you to making substantial savings over the cost of working from commercial premises.

Lighting can be kept to a minimum by arranging your workspace to take maximum advantage of no-cost natural light, using additional lighting only when necessary. You will perhaps have to provide additional heating above what you would normally use in the home if you went out to work, but again you can at least control what you use. You needn't heat the whole house or flat; just the room in which you are working, turning it off when it reaches a comfortable working temperature; in the early part of your working day you will be able to take advantage of the residual heat from the morning's regular warm-through.

You might have been more aware of these savings if you had moved from rented premises into your home. For the person starting out at home these may be 'hidden' savings – but they will still be making themselves felt in your cashflow, perhaps even making the difference between whether you have to take out a business loan or not. But the real advantage comes in being able to feed these savings through to your customers and/or your business. This might be your first step in turning your consciousness towards being entrepreneurial and exercising your business acumen: making decisions which are for the benefit of your business; being aware of the real impact of your actions and decisions; keeping the cashflow in focus; budgeting; watching overheads; staying in control; and managing your work environment effectively.

## Utilizing Assets

Big businesses always keep an eye on their assets and make sure they are working for them, whether by stashing away excess funds in off-shore accounts or by making full use of the skills within their workforce.

By working at home you too will be making use of one of your assets – the place you live. In a full-time job you may only make use of it 14 or 15 hours or less a day; the same if you run your business from commercial premises. For the rest of the time your home may be lying empty, dormant. When you work from home you are making your home work for you in the fullest way possible. Only a business fool would let such an asset underperform.

Items in the home can also be realized as working assets, including claiming as a tax-deductible expense those things which have been in domestic use and which can now be put to multi-use instead. For example, part of the telephone rental costs can now be claimed as a business expense. Instead of it sitting there during the day and not, as it were, earning its keep, you can now put it to full use – and receive the financial advantage of doing so. Check with your accountant or local tax office about the other items you can use and claim against tax.

## Travel Costs

One of the first benefits to be felt by someone starting to work from home is that the daily trek to work becomes a thing of the past. As a result, many savings can be made instantly:

- no more costly season tickets
- lower petrol bills (perhaps you were one of those commuters who joined the fuel-consuming traffic jams twice a day?)
- less wear and tear on the car and therefore fewer repair bills
- lower mileage, meaning your car will probably need to be replaced less frequently – and command a higher price when it does
- as one homeworker, Hal, points out, you may even be able to claim a discount on your car insurance if you become a low-mileage car user
- you might even consider whether you need a car at all now; might peddle- or foot-power be sufficient?
- the need for a second family car might now disappear
- part of the costs of running the car can now be claimed as a tax-deductible expense

These are all benefits which work to your and your business' advantage.

## Increasing the Family's Income

The need to improve the family's income might be high on the list of reasons why you want to start a business from home. On the other hand, you may be looking at ways to develop a hobby or make better use of your free time. In this case you might be pleasantly surprised that by putting your leisure pursuits on a professional footing you can now generate a second income, either by supplementing your own as the main wage earner or by contributing to the bulk of the family's budget.

What starts out as a mini-enterprise may well develop into something which provides you or your family with a more secure financial future and a regular additional income. In addition to the obvious advantages to your family, this income might also be a way of developing your own sense of independence.

In these unpredictable times it might be wise to have a 'belt and braces' approach to securing the family's fortunes. If the main wage-earning job were to disappear through unexpected redundancy, at least your home business would provide a financial fall-back position, greatly reducing the impact of such a blow.

### Other Financial Advantages

By working at home, child-minding fees can be kept to a minimum and perhaps may not be needed at all. This can represent a huge saving to the family budget. Where being in a job may have meant that child-minding was an unavoidable cost, you can make a significant saving straight away, ploughing back the money saved into the family in other ways, or using it to benefit your business and its customers.

Another advantage which feeds indirectly into savings has been pointed out to me by Hal, who soon realized for himself that he no longer had to dress up for work every day. I too have found that I spend less money on maintaining a comprehensive 'work' wardrobe of clothes. I still need a couple of outfits, but the range has now shrunk to fit in with the fewer times I now have to attend any business-linked appointments. For anyone whose job in the past has demanded a high standard of dress and whose new business dictates otherwise, the savings in this area alone can be significant.

Money can also be saved by taking advantage of being able to holiday and travel outside of peak periods.

Because you are working at home, cheap nutritious lunches can easily be made to replace costly shop-bought food.

## ■ USE OF TIME

### Self-directed Routines

Regardless of whether you feel like it or not, come Monday morning your boss expects you to turn up and be willing to get on with your job of work. You are expected to get on with whatever he or she wants you to do, ignoring the fact that really you would be much better this morning doing some quiet filing for an hour or so. Instilling work practices and getting people to respond to the ongoing demands of the work situation was one of the problems encountered by factory managers at the beginning of the Industrial Revolution. Peasant farmers who came to the towns for jobs had been used to working according to the dictates of their own needs and desires, and it proved a difficult exercise for some to turn up to work regularly and on time in order to do a day's work, every working day. Perhaps there's still that note of resistance and unwillingness to be subjugated to other's whims in many of us.

When you're working at home, indeed working in any self-employed capacity, you are much more able to direct your own routines, taking breaks when you want to – not when you're allowed or told to. When asked about the advantages of working at home, William says, 'Working when I want. I'm an early morning person and I get a lot of work done between seven and nine o'clock in the morning. I also like picking work up – and putting it down – when I want.' Carol also identifies this as an advantage. 'When I'm working towards a deadline I can sit up far into the night or get up really early and work in my dressing gown.' When you're in employment it is much more difficult to make use of your energy and interest patterns, especially if they occur outside normal working hours.

Hilary also finds that her routines can be fitted in with how she feels, and finds herself 'working different hours depending on my mood'. Some days you may spend 15 hours solid at work; on others you may put in just an hour or two and spend the rest of the time in the park. The control of when and how you work rests with yourself when you're running your own show. 'You work when you like and can stop as early or as late as your work and social life permit,' confirms Charles. (More about this later in the book.)

## Travel Time

A friend of mine used to travel about 350 miles a day going to and from work. Apart from the incredibly high cost, it also meant his day was extended by two to two-and-a-half hours, at either end. He said that it wasn't too bad once you got into the routine, but I could only think 'what an awful waste of time'. (So did he in the end: he is now living and working happily in France!)

Although this may be an extreme example it is not unusual for commuters to spend well over two hours each day just getting to their place of work and back again. This means that for an average commuter extra time equivalent to one-and-a-quarter working days is spent travelling every week. When you're working at home the advantage of not having to squander these huge chunks of time becomes immediately apparent. No sooner have you finished breakfast or perhaps taken the kids to school, when there you are, at your desk, ready to start.

This time-saving advantage can be ploughed back into either family or social time – or back into your business to increase your productivity. Or it can, of course, simply be relished.

## Flexibility

Because you are able to direct your own routines, it also follows that your time becomes more flexible. This gives you the advantage of being able to accommodate any domestic or personal arrangements such as being in for the plumber or having to go to the dentist. It can also mean that it becomes easier to make such arrangements, since you are able to book them for less busy appointment hours. As Gilly says, 'Working from home eases the demands of home management.'

This flexibility also allows you to holiday out of peak season when you always run into the possible danger of finding as much hassle and as many crowds as those you endeavoured to leave behind in the city. I never leave town on holiday weekends, having spent too many of them sitting in traffic jams along with all the other hopefuls, only to end up exhausted and bad tempered at the end of it. Instead, I've discovered just how quiet and lovely the city can be when everyone's left, and I reserve my holiday weekends for other times – when breaks are often a lot cheaper, too. You can even have your 'weekend' midweek –

taking advantage of lower transport and hotel charges – and make up the work you miss at the real weekend.

## Benefits to Others

Because of your own flexibility others may benefit as well. It may be possible to reorganize household chores which, without putting you to any inconvenience, frees some of your partner's time. It may be possible for you to become more involved in your children's activities, for instance, including taking them to school and attending parents' evenings and school performances where previously this may have been difficult to arrange. Everyone benefits from you being able to spend more time with them, and it provides you with the opportunity to become a more active and involved member of your family.

On the business level, David points out a significant advantage of this flexibility: 'It means I can be available to answer calls more or less 24 hours a day.' This may not be what everyone wants when they're in business, but in his work as a natural health practitioner he sees it as important. It also means that he can pick up business long after other practitioners have shut up shop for the day or weekend. For you, too, this may be the difference between getting that all-important next client or not.

## Lifestyle

Working from home means different lifestyles become possible. The nine-to-five imposes its restrictions on us and therefore inevitably dictates to a large degree how we live our lives for the greater part of the week. Once free of these restrictions you can create a better style of living more in keeping with what you really want.

We've already mentioned the time and money saved in

travel costs, but you also no longer have to face the stresses, strains and inconvenience commuting brings with it. Instead, you now have the opportunity to build some regular exercise into the extra time available, and even take time out to go swimming or have a regular therapeutic massage.

You also have the chance to revamp your eating habits. Instead of one coffee break and a half-hour for lunch, you can have small nutritious snacks throughout your day, if you like, or treat yourself to a leisurely hot lunch – it's up to you.

You can be more yourself. No need to duck and dive among the power games at work. You can dress how you like and find work routines to suit your psychology. You can also be there for your children instead of having to feel guilty about them or about leaving your partner to handle them all the time. It all adds up to less stress.

Barry makes it sound almost like a holiday:

*Virtually everything I might need for writing is here, but if I get fed up with writing everything I need to relax is also here – tea, food, television, videos, even light fiction and a bottle of wine. I also have no rush hour, no getting up early and no boss. I choose my own working hours, which can be from 11 a.m. to 1 a.m. And being a writer, I can work in the lounge, or even in the garden in summer. It's very pleasant 'work'!*

Starting to work from home will mean a major change; with it comes the chance to create a lifestyle more in keeping with what suits you and what you really want out of life.

## ▪ WORK ENVIRONMENT

When we accept a job we also have to accept the physical

working conditions which go with it and which we rarely have much influence over. I've already recounted the story of my nightmare workplace and I'm sure many others have memories and experiences which compare. Fortunately, when you work at home you have the advantage of being able to create a working environment to suit you. Even if it is only a corner space to start off with, you can choose *which* corner and make it as appealing as you want. After all, you are working in your own home which will presumably be decorated and furnished according to your tastes anyway. You're already going to feel the benefit of that rather than having to put up with the ghastly greying walls found in a lot of workplaces. If you have the money, you may want to consider having a custom-made office space designed for your home, using one of the companies that specialize in this (listed in the *Yellow Pages* under 'Furniture Designers').

When asked about the advantages of working from home, Alice cites the joy of being in her home environment, being able 'to sit in the window in the sunshine and paint. Very therapeutic; very satisfying. And being able to listen to the radio as I work.' Working at home can be psychologically more comfortable, and if you're feeling good about where you are, you will work better. Similarly, Gilly says that one of the spin-offs for her is an improvement in her quality of life, since she is now able to work in rural surroundings which benefit her sense of well-being.

On a more practical note, Hal points out that 'because of the high crime rate, you're also at home to protect your own stuff – it saves on burglar alarms!' Looking to the growing trend of homeworkers in general, including teleworkers, homes with adapted office space may now start to command premium prices, giving you an advantage should you ever want to sell your home and move to another.

Where you work is important; working at home you have the advantage of being able to create your own individual environment, one which lends itself to your own particular business needs and personal preferences.

## ▪ IMPROVED PRODUCTIVITY

Comparisons between office-based workers and teleworkers show that teleworkers are more productive. People working away from the many distractions of office life appear to be able to get through a greater volume of work – four times as much according to a joint CBI and BT conference in the UK in 1988. The advantage to you is that this will directly affect the competitive edge of your business. You will be able to turn round orders or fulfil contracts that much more quickly, increasing your profits. When this happens you will be reaping the rewards for yourself rather than the anonymous corporate boss or shareholders.

Ceasing to commute can reveal another benefit: not only will you have the previous commuting time to yourself, you will also have the energy which would otherwise have been used in simply getting yourself to work and back. And when the weather, severe traffic hold-ups or strikes affect others getting to work, you have the advantage of being able to carry on as normal. Your competitors might not be able to function with only a skeleton crew, whereas you're operating as normal, ready to pick up and action the next sales enquiry.

## ▪ PERSONAL GAINS

There are also personal gains to be made from working for yourself at home. Carol says she has felt an increase in her levels of confidence and also in her status – now as a freelance journalist. Derek says that it feels 'great to be my own boss – taking and being responsible for my own decisions'. It can certainly give your morale a real boost to turn your kitchen table into the thriving hub of a successful business operation, knowing that you've done it yourself. And by finding your own particular niche in which to be successful, your own sense of identity is given the opportunity to develop instead of being limited to the status of just another number on the payroll, or to chief cook and bottle washer.

You might, because of a unique combination of these advantages, just generally feel happier with yourself – perhaps the best spin-off of all.

## ▪ THE ENVIRONMENT AND SOCIETY

By deciding to work from home you will be joining many others who, through their individual actions, will also be benefiting the environment and society at large – though probably not through any conscious intent.

If you previously used your car to go to work, by staying at home you will now be helping to ameliorate the problems of atmospheric pollution caused by car fumes. And because there is one less car on the road there will be one less car in the traffic queue. Who knows, the disappearance of your car might be the one to bring the queue to an end, further helping against pollution since stationary and slow-moving cars cause the most problems. Even if the queue doesn't disappear, you will still be helping to relieve congestion in your area and the one you travelled to.

Fewer hours spent on the road will also decrease the possibility of being in an accident.

More workers at home will certainly have an effect at community level. This is something which Gilly noticed when she started working from home and which became an added and very unexpected bonus when she realized she had gained 'immediate access to the local community. Belonging to the area in which I live. You're noticed,' she says, 'suddenly you're no longer a transient character who goes out to work.' Areas which once became dead and vacant when people went out to work may be revitalized as acquaintances are made and local networks formed.

You will probably find yourself spending more money locally than you might have done before. This too is beneficial for a community. The more times money circulates within an area, the wealthier it becomes. By basing yourself at home you are unwittingly helping to develop and maintain a thriving community. Your order to a local printer might be the one to tip the financial balance and enable a new job to be created, perhaps for a young apprentice.

Your decision to work from home will bring benefits to you, your family and your business. Some of them have been mentioned here; there may also be others for you personally to realize. Even beyond the confines of your home there may be surprising advantages for others; people who might least expect them – or who might remain totally unaware of where these pluses are coming from.

# 4 ▪ Practical Issues

Being aware of the advantages of working from home is important, but it would give an unbalanced and unrealistic picture not to have a look at some of the practical issues. In looking at these I don't mean to be the proverbial wet blanket; it is just to give you the opportunity to consider what might lie ahead and prepare yourself beforehand. By identifying any potential areas of difficulty before you start and addressing the issues in advance, then time, money, efficiency and – not least of all – your frayed nerves can all be saved. Foreseeing problems and taking evasive action is surely one of the hallmarks of a successful manager; and learning how to manage your own enterprise successfully is probably top of your list of priorities. Fortunately, instead of waiting for the difficulties to emerge you can gain some valuable insights through the experience of others who have already been there, seen it and, unfortunately, done it.

## ▪ IMAGE OF HOMEWORKING

You have the qualifications, experience, facilities and enthusiasm. But one thing you do *not* have in working at home is an upmarket business address and location. You know this will have no effect on the quality of your work, but others might assume that because you're operating out of the garden shed your business is amateurish and your work unprofessional.

This sort of attitude appears to be cultural. Simon, who has worked in the US in a self-employed capacity from his home-base there, makes a comparison with the attitude of clients in the UK:

*Clients in the States are more geared up to using people who work from home. They even provide you with access to secretarial support. You don't have to hide the fact that you're working from home. In this country there's still a stigma.*

With the growth in self-employment and in the number of those who work from home, perhaps this attitude may be changing. Employers themselves are now establishing teleworking schemes so that employees can work from home, and perhaps this too might help to reinforce a more positive perception of home-based workers. The sweat-shop image of low-paid, cheap labour previously associated with homeworkers is gradually being left behind as greater numbers of professional people join the ranks. The more that clients become familiar with seeing people working from home in a professional capacity, and the more it becomes a common feature of working practice, the less suspect it will seem to them. But it takes time for new styles of working to be absorbed into the professional culture anywhere. Until then, although you will find many clients happy with the fact that you work from home, there may still be others who remain sceptical and who pre-judge you and your business professionalism. You must be prepared for the possibility that some prospective clients may even decide to take their business elsewhere.

## Ensuring a Professional Image

If you want your clients to feel comfortable with the idea that you work from home, it is important that you yourself feel comfortable with it too. You don't want to give the impression that you are being evasive about your business location and where you operate from, lest your clients think you have something to hide – perhaps something about the legality of what you are doing or even your full commitment to your business and clients. Neither does a jokey approach come across well. It still implies a glossing-over, a less than direct and therefore slightly dishonest attitude. Clients and customers will equate that with how you operate.

An honest, open, direct and non-defensive attitude about your place of work leaves little to the imagination about whether your operation is suspect or not. For you to be able to take this stance you need to feel comfortable about it yourself. Take time to reflect on any reservations you might have and any worries you might be harbouring about how your prospective clients might react to your business location. Face these worries, address them and accept that being defensive or trying to hide the fact that you work from home will only be picked up by clients and reflected back on yourself and your business.

Should you find customers voicing concerns, or if you detect any hesitancy, you can only attempt to reassure them of your utmost professionalism, your skills and your experience (let them know if this has developed in a commercial environment, especially if you used to work for a renowned company). Make use of any references and quotes you might have from satisfied customers. It can be tricky to do all this without lapsing into the defensive mode; you might have to practise delivering these reassurances in a calm, assertive manner. Enlist the help of someone to play the part of a reluctant or wary customer to help you work out the best voice and stock phrases to use. If you don't feel comfortable with that, practise with a cassette recorder – or even in front of a video camera if you have one at home or can borrow one. It will be useful for you to hear and/or see how you come across and you will probably be able to pick up quite easily on any defensive inflection in your voice. You might have to give yourself regular practice sessions until you feel confident enough.

Remember: If you are confident about yourself and your situation, the greater the likelihood that your client will be, too.

Your image is also carried across via your business literature, which should be the best quality you can afford in terms of design and production. But even with the most professional-looking letterheads your residential address might cause a problem, particularly if you live in a flat. Addresses tend to be written in full: *Flat 5, 62 The Road, Old Town*. You may like to consider adopting the style used in other countries: *5/62 The Road, Old Town*, which is less obvious and may indicate an office rather than a residential block. Pop along to your local postal sorting office to check that adopting this style won't cause problems for them. The last thing you want is for your mail to disappear to number *562*, or *5162*. If you don't want to indicate a flat number or letter at all, have a word with the sorting office about dropping it and having your business name as your address. Instead of *Flat 5*, your letters could then simply be addressed to *Working Well Associates*.

If you live in a house there's less of a problem, unless it has a name which is inappropriate for your business. *Rose Cottage* wouldn't be too bad if you make country crafts, but it might not give the right impression if your business is in exports or your clients are blue-chip organizations. Again, your postal sorting office will advise you about making any house name changes, including giving your house a business name instead of a house number. But be careful what you choose: the magnificent sounding *Corporate House* might invite only scorn when your client (being led to expect a grand establishment) visits your small terraced house. It's not that there is anything wrong with the fact that you're running your business from a terraced house, but you might be seen as trying to mislead your customers. So don't be too pretentious. It smacks of dishonesty, and potential clients may be wary.

Also, think carefully before using a Post Office or other mailing address box number. Many people are suspicious about businesses which have these as their operational address. Understandably it looks as if you really do have something to hide – and people will decide for themselves what that might be. On the other hand you might like to investigate using a business service address, although it will mean you have to make special journeys to collect your mail. However, by using a business centre's facilities you might then have access to other facilities, like meeting rooms.

## Meetings with Clients

Some businesses are conducted without any face-to-face contact with customers or clients, such as mail order businesses. In this case the prospect of handling meetings at home is unlikely to arise. For others, it may be the professional norm to meet at the client's office or customer's home. However, yours may be a business in which meeting clients is an integral part of your work.

If you feel uncomfortable with the prospect, or if you live in a remote and largely inaccessible place, you could suggest alternative meeting places – perhaps somewhere for lunch, morning coffee, afternoon tea or an early evening drink. If you are a member of a golf club or something similar you might also consider carrying on your business in this more informal setting – depending of course on the nature of that business.

If these alternatives aren't available or appropriate you might like to consider hiring a meeting room or small conference room in a hotel, conference centre or business services centre. Again, you might have to practise making these suggestions to clients. Edges of defensiveness or avoidance tactics need to be eliminated or else you could come across as being rather shifty.

## Meetings at Home

There may be times when a meeting at your home is the only option. The success or failure of this will depend on you as much as on your preparation. Your client needs to feel confident and at ease in what may be an unfamiliar situation, and will take his or her cue from how *you* act.

Some of your confidence will come from knowing you have prepared well. Here are a few tips:

- Decide where the meeting should take place: in your workspace, living room or dining room.
- Make sure the seating is arranged properly.
- Clear away family and household clutter, not only in the meeting room but also in the hallway, stairs, bathroom or anywhere else the client may have to pass through.
- Close the doors to the other rooms in the house.
- Eliminate any lingering cooking smells.
- Make sure the front garden is tidy.
- Prepare your documents, papers and materials and have them ready to hand.
- Have some tea, coffee and a soft drink ready to offer. You may want to consider providing yourself with facilities to do this in your meeting room to save having to abandon your client while you go and fuss round the kitchen.
- Turn on the answering machine 10–15 minutes beforehand, or have someone ready to answer the phone on the second ring in another room. If none of these is possible, consider

whether to unplug the phone (although you run the risk of missing important calls). Perhaps the easiest option is to have your phone to hand and to act as any other office-based worker would when the phone rings: excuse yourself to your client, answer promptly, tell the caller you are in a meeting and take his or her name and number to call back afterwards (even if it's little Tommy phoning for Susie).

- Choose a time of day for the meeting when you are least likely to have other household members around. If necessary, and possible, arrange for children to be out of the house.
- If people are going to be about, brief everyone in the household carefully about the time and likely duration of the meeting. Agree with them a 'Code of Behaviour' while meetings are in progress, including the following points:

  - no phone calls if the phone is within hearing distance of the meeting room
  - no interruptions
  - if anyone has to enter or leave the house, he or she should try to use the back door
  - all internal doors should be kept closed (and closing them quietly in the first place!)
  - no music, radio or television (again, if these can be heard from the room in which you are having your meeting) until after the meeting has finished
  - no friends over to visit just then – they are welcome to visit another time
  - no cooking. Smells and pan-rattling are intrusive and distracting.

So, prepared and ready, you should be able to greet your client with confidence. Resist any temptation to apologize for the fact that you are meeting in your home. Act professionally, direct your client to the meeting room, offer the refreshments and get stuck into the business in hand. When the client sees how professionally and confidently you handle the meeting and yourself in this 'home' situation, he or she will feel 100 per cent reassured about giving you his or her business.

## ▪ SPACE

An oft-cited problem with working from home is that of space. Tell me about it: I have worked tucked away in a corner space not much larger than a metre square. I'd be lying if I said that was an ideal solution – it wasn't. But it was the only one available to me at the time, and if I hadn't put down my working roots there I probably wouldn't be writing this now.

I'm sure that for many others the corner of the kitchen table is where it all starts. Yes, it is less than perfect, but if it is a case of using that or not getting your business off the ground at all, then the choice is clear.

What carried me through was keeping firmly in my mind what my exit strategy was and how I was going to get there. I never lost sight of that and somehow it made working in those cramped conditions more bearable because I knew clearly why I was doing it: I was working towards my goal of financial independence.

If space is tight, it might help you to plan your own exit strategy. According to your business plan, how long will it be before you can acquire more space? How are you going to do that? By building an extension? converting a garage, basement or attic space? adding a conservatory? buying out the other mortgagee? being patient until one of your children leaves home? building an outhouse? hiring storage space? installing a professionally designed, custom-made, dedicated workspace? renting office space outside your home?

Knowing what your next step is going to be may help you to keep your present space difficulties in perspective rather than being tempted to throw everything over in exasperation. Work out what your own personal space plans are for the future and the steps you have to take to get there.

In the meantime, do what you can to make the space situation more bearable. Here are some tips:

- Check you are not letting papers and documents which could be put into storage take up valuable working space.
- Pin-boards are useful for keeping important notes to hand. I made mine out of six cork tiles stuck to the wall – much cheaper than any shop-bought version, and a lot nicer than most.
- Invest in one or two two-drawer filing cabinets to help keep your papers in order. By putting a board across them you have instant desk space as well.
- Desk and drawer tidies are essential for helping you make the most of available space.
- What use can you make of any wall space? Shelves and cabinets can be put up to boost the space you have. Look at different sizes of shelves. Deeper ones can provide the answer to storing larger documents, materials or samples.
- What about the ceiling? Suspended shelves, storage platforms and baskets can all free up that little bit of extra room in which to manoeuvre.
- Go for a browse around DIY, garden and stationery stores. You might discover some new products to answer your storage and workspace problems and enable you to organize yourself more efficiently, such as stackable open plastic storage crates or stackable desk-trays.

- Trolleys are useful for providing additional work-surfaces and storage space which can easily be moved out of the way.
- Arrange your workspace so that it is out of your line of vision when you're not working. My square metre of space was in my bedroom so I placed it behind where I slept. When I was relaxing before going to sleep at least I couldn't see my work; neither did it greet me first thing in the morning.
- Invest in a screen or blind to close off your work area once you've finished for the day.
- If you really are having to work off the kitchen table and it's causing difficulties, have another good look around to see if you can't spot some other space which you could use instead. What you want is a dedicated area in which you can leave your papers and work set out and not have to clear them away at the end of every day. Look for spaces in the hallway; under the stairs; behind doors; a corner which could be screened off; a walk-in or built-in cupboard to build a desk into; a high room which could have 'balcony' space built into it.

## ■ FACILITIES

It can come as a surprise when you leave 'The Organization' and start to work for yourself that the facilities you have previously taken for granted are now no longer accessible to you. Photo-copiers seem to come high on the list of 'Things I Miss Most' for a lot of people who were previously office-based. Fax machines also seem to be pined for by quite a few. 'Not having access to a photocopier and "free" phones is a real pain,' confesses Hal, 'although they're not that big a problem.' His solution is to use clients' own equipment when he can, otherwise, like many of us, he uses the photocopier in the shop down the road.

It can be inconvenient having to make a special trip to copy some papers, and it does take you away from your work. Before you succumb to the temptation of buying your own, however, run a tally of just how many copies you do in a month. Also make a note of how much time it takes, over a month, to go and get them done. Now that you are working for yourself your time is valuable and you need to make sure you are using it economically. Cost all this out and compare it with the cost of buying a small, portable copier of your own. If your usage is relatively high, renting a low-volume desk-top model might be a better and cheaper option.

If your nearest copier is located some distance away, you might consider encouraging a local shop or library to install one. They might need some convincing: producing your figures and those of other homeworkers in the area will help your argument. Failing that, you could try negotiating with a nearby small business for the use of their machine.

The same arguments apply to fax machines which, like photocopiers, have come down significantly in price over the years. Cost it out and you may be surprised to find that buying your own is the most sensible option.

Besides lack of facilities, inadequate ones can also be a problem. Gerald finds this true of his telephone, admitting that 'there is occasional congestion on the telephone since there is no separate line for my office.' Although you are trying to keep costs down, especially when setting up in business, you need also to consider the benefit of having another line installed. If it means losing sales because callers can't get through to you (Auntie Flo has been on the phone for half an hour – again), then it becomes a false economy *not* to have one installed.

There is another benefit to be gained from having a dedicated business line, too. It makes it easier for other members of the household to know when it is a business call that is coming through, and also whether they should answer or not. At the end of your business day it also makes it easier to keep work-related calls from impinging on your social time. The answer machine can handle callers out of office hours until the following day. When all calls have to come through on the one line it makes it difficult not to be caught by a client just when you're sitting down to dinner. It is another expense, but having a separate line installed can bring with it many benefits and pay for itself in many different ways. Having said that, your decision of course depends on your business. For example, as a writer it is less of a problem for me, but Gilly finds it difficult in her import business to have to deal with calls from both suppliers and customers late into the evening.

## ▪INTERRUPTIONS

We all tend to suffer from these whether we are in a job of work or self-employed at home. To that extent they are going to happen regardless and losing your temper is perhaps in part a result of not coming to terms with the fact. However, even if you can't eliminate interruptions entirely you can try to minimize their number and also develop 'damage limitation' strategies for dealing with them when they do occur.

You might have to embark on an education programme. I suppose it is unfair to expect friends or household members to know when it is or is not OK to interrupt with a phone call or visit. It's up to you to draft your own guidelines to suit your hours, nature of work and so on. I let friends know when I'm going 'incommunicado' to finish a manuscript, then switch on the answering machine, close the door and hope people remember and respect my time constraints until I've finished.

With a more regular work-pattern it should be easier to let

people know when you can and cannot be disturbed. You might choose to make it a blanket rule that between 9 a.m. and 6 p.m. you are to be regarded as 'out to work'. This can be difficult to instil in some people, who may not accept that you are serious in your venture. Gilly has encountered 'a lack of understanding from people who may just drop in, insinuating that you're just "resting"'. Her answer to the problem has been 'to educate people as to the nature of self-employment, motivation and working from home.' She continues:

*Family and friends took my business as a joke initially and didn't take me seriously. I don't ever want to take myself so seriously that I can't have a laugh, but I think you're easy prey to snide comments and the like. You're very vulnerable in the early days to any insidious remarks. I really had to draw on my past managerial experience and social skills. The rule of thumb for me is to play it down.*

Reflecting on why there can be this certain lack of respect for what you are doing, Gilly thinks:

*Perhaps the comments are because you've rocked the boat by becoming self-employed. Their defence is to rock you back and see you frightened and unsuccessful, because you're challenging their status quo and what they're doing or not doing with their own lives.*

Simon had similar experiences with his former wife, who found it difficult getting to grips with the fact that he 'wasn't there'. 'Spontaneous interruptions were always happening despite having talks about it – she'd always do it again later.' He now sees that there were other undercurrents present and that her interruptions were one manifestation of her not wanting him to succeed.

If you suspect that people are not trying very hard to respect your wishes, you might find yourself having to face and sort out the more difficult underlying issues. More of this in Chapter 8 – in the meantime, it is down to you to establish your work routines and let people know when you can and cannot be interrupted.

Strategies for Minimizing Interruptions:

- Keep your office door closed.
- Make sure household members understand what the closed door means.
- Indicate on the door when you will be free – if they can see they've only half an hour to wait they'll be more accommodating.
- Remove any spare chairs in your office, to discourage any lingering chats.
- If you're working in a family room, put coloured cubes on your work surface or pin up coloured paper to signal when it is OK to interrupt what you're doing; green for yes, red for 'at your peril'.
- Position yourself so that your back faces people. If they are tempted to pop their head round the door, and see you bent over your work, they will be less inclined to interrupt.
- Ignore the mail deliveries. Don't be tempted to interrupt what you are doing to open letters. They can wait until your present task is finished, otherwise you could well be sidetracked into responding to communications straight away.

Damage Limitation:

- Telephone interruptions: say you are in a meeting and that you will ring back later. When you do, you might want to remind the caller about when you can take casual calls.

- Beat them to it – before they start talking, tell them kindly but firmly that you do not want to be interrupted right now.
- Use your body language to reinforce the message that the interruption is not welcome. As soon as you move in response to them they will subconsciously read that as having won your attention and will carry on. When you break contact with your work and make eye contact with them, they're in.
- Just as you have learned how to act confidently about welcoming clients to your home, you may have to practise being assertive and saying 'No' firmly and confidently to interruptions.

Interruptions will happen, but as you learn to handle them more confidently you may feel less threatened or upset by them when they do occur. Try to accept that both you and your family and friends will probably have to go through a learning curve on this one.

## ■ DISTRACTIONS

'I find it easy to become distracted,' confesses William, 'so last-minute late-night work often takes place.' Distractions can be enjoyable, but if they become too protracted the consequences often create problems.

It helps to remove potential distractors from view, like the morning paper or domestic bills which need paying. On your desk, clear to one side any papers except the ones you're working on; keep business magazines and the like out of sight.

The rest of the battle seems to rest with your own sense of self-discipline. The difficulty may lie in the fact that you are expecting yourself to work for periods of time which are too long. Try giving yourself a five-minute break every 40 minutes or so. You might find that the distractions were simply your subconscious' way of telling you that you were ready for a break. You might also find exercising during the day helps. Sedentary work can leave you with excess physical energy to be burned off. Restlessness and being easily distracted go hand in hand.

In my experience distractions don't work unless I want them to, like when I'm struggling with a chapter or dealing with material which is boring but essential. Distractions are my way of finding an escape from something I don't want to do.

If having regular breaks or exercise doesn't work, and distractions are proving to be a deep and continuing problem, you may have to address the issue of what you are avoiding in your work. You may be trying to force yourself to work at something which isn't really you, or you might find that with working alone your day is long enough after six hours or so. Read on to Chapter 8.

## ▪ MULTI-SKILLING

You have set up a business which makes or deals in widgets. You understand widgets and know everything there is to know about them. It is your love of widgets that is your reason for going into business. Unfortunately there are other aspects to running your own show at home, which quickly become apparent.

Previously you might never have had to think about secretarial work – it was always handled by someone else. Now you have to be your own receptionist, typist, filing clerk, postal clerk and stationery monitor. Accounts were always sorted by Head Office, but now you have to deal with everything from petty cash to invoicing, VAT and budgeting. Suddenly you realize you're on your own. Marketing your business is your responsibility as well.

Making your widgets becomes only one, albeit vital aspect of your business.

Gilly soon felt the impact when she started working from home: 'I was struck by the lack of available skills to draw upon from a department of personnel.' Now your department is just you. William found this aspect of working from home the most problematical:

> It's the administration, VAT and paperwork which is the most difficult thing to cope with, and I am getting very close to getting someone to help me a few days a month. If I could reduce my workload I could, hopefully, schedule it all much easier at home, and find time to teach myself how to use my new word processor. I've had it for nine months and still haven't touched it. So much for trying to streamline my business!

Working for yourself can be a good opportunity to expand your range of skills. In the early days it may appear you have little option. But if you find you don't take easily to the new demands, you may have to consider alternatives. It won't really prove to be beneficial to your business if you end up spending two days sorting out some simple filing, or typing a few letters. That time could be better spent by you completing an order or drumming up new sales. Training might be an option for you to consider; using available help is another. Read on to Chapters 6 and 7.

## ▪BREAKS FROM THE BUSINESS

When there's only you running your business, taking a break from it can prove difficult. After a fortnight's absence on holiday you run the risk of everything grinding to a halt, and without careful planning it could take your business up to three weeks to recover after your return from a two-week break. One homeworker tried taking breaks separately from her husband so that there was always some cover. It might solve the problem for your business but it's hardly good for marital harmony. Managing long breaks is a problem common to many self-employed people.

Devising a coping strategy is vital if you don't want your business to come to a complete standstill.

Here are some suggestions:

- Use your answering machine message to let people know when you will be back in the office again.
- Contact your customers to let them know the dates of your absence and how you might be contacted during that time – if you want to be.
- You might like to think about leaving a forwarding telephone number on the telephone message. You will have to balance whether you want to take calls while you are on holiday against the risk of losing customers.
- Consider having your calls re-directed to a telephone answering service.
- Training someone to business-sit in your absence might be your best bet. It will have to be someone you can trust since they will be in your home, but even if they can only be available to cover for half a day, at least it provides a basic service to clients and customers.
- The cost of hiring a temp for a few hours a day to cover calls needs to be balanced against the benefit to your customers and the level of customer care you provide them with.
- Sales enquiries can be fielded by your helper or temp by having literature available for them to send out.

- Accept that in these early days your holidays might have to be shorter, say a week instead of two, and that since you are the business you might have to take it with you on your 'break'.
- Read on to Chapter 7.

## ▪ PERSONAL SAFETY

You could be particularly vulnerable if you live alone and your business involves contact with lots of clients. Without meaning to be a scaremonger, it is only sensible for me to advise you to take some simple precautions for your own safety, particularly when you have to meet new clients.

It may be wise to make your initial meeting on neutral territory. When you are making the appointment, take the client's full name, address and telephone number, and phone back to check the details are correct. Leave a note in your desk diary with these details and where the meeting is taking place.

If the meeting is to take place in either your home or the client's, go through the same procedure for checking their credentials. You can do so without highlighting your anxieties, by masking it as a confirmation of the meeting – a normal business procedure. Once you have met the client and are satisfied that he or she is bona fide, you need not go to such lengths again, although it is always wise to keep full details of all appointments in your diary.

If you feel particularly vulnerable in your home you could consider having a 'panic' button installed as an extension to a burglar alarm system. And learning some simple self-defence is perhaps something we should all do. Now might be a good time for you to sign up for those classes.

In the UK, a study on homeworking carried out for the Department of Employment (1987) looked into the disadvantages of working from home for the homeworker. We have had a look at some of these here. But you might find that you fall into the 28 per cent of people for whom there were no disadvantages at all to working at home. And by raising your awareness about potential areas of difficulty you should be able to take evasive action and boost that figure even further.

## 5 ▪ *So-lo Working — When Things Don't Feel Too Good*

We've had a look at some of the more practical and operational difficulties which can emerge when you're working at home, but what can sometimes be more distressing is finding yourself up against challenges which are more personal in their nature. These are the problems which can severely affect you and your work and undermine your basic enjoyment of being a home-worker.

### ▪ LONELINESS

Perhaps understandably, studies show that people who work at home can experience feelings of isolation and loneliness. The bustling office, which may have angered you in the past, is now looked back on with nostalgia and fondness. You might surprise yourself by discovering that you miss it, yearning for the company you once found so irksome. If you have previously worked in that kind of environment you might have to resign yourself to undergoing a period of transition in which you adjust to your new, quieter and calmer place of work. It might seem unsettling at first, but perhaps it might help to reassure yourself that it is simply the stark contrast between your previous workplace and your new one at home which you need to give yourself time to adjust to.

## Social Animals

Having said that, human beings are social animals. Some need more interaction with people than others, but we certainly all need it. Being with people provides us with more than just someone to share a cup of tea with; it satisfies some of our instinctive, emotional needs in life.

At the most basic level, being with people satisfies our need for recognition. We need to experience acknowledgement from others that we exist. Further up the scale we search for a more sophisticated sort of recognition concerning who we are and what tasks we are working on. Our sense of well-being depends on receiving approval; that we are OK and that what we are doing is OK, too. We need to feel these strokes from others, since we've been conditioned from birth to expect and receive them. Those initial experiences, deep in our memories, recall the sense of comfort and security which being with people brought us when we were babes in arms. Loneliness is an emotional response to being apart from the people from whom we receive these positive strokes.

Feeling lonely for extended periods can be harmful, so it is an area which needs to be addressed, especially if it is a real, ongoing problem or if you think it might become one the longer you work at home.

We all feel lonely at some time or other. It might provide some reassurance to remember that fact. Because you're feeling lonely doesn't mean that you are a social outcast or an oddity. It means that you are sharing an experience which everyone has every now and again. If you're feeling lonely now, you can bet your last lire that there are hundreds of other homeworkers feeling exactly the same, and others who will feel like this tomorrow – perhaps when your feelings have changed.

## An Opportunity

Feeling lonely is an opportunity to discover something more about your own personal and unique needs. When you work in a busy environment with lots of other people around, personal needs tend to become modified in order to make the whole situation workable for everyone. You have to play at give and take. When you work on your own, it's possible that your own needs start to clamour for attention because there's no reason now why they should be quashed; and as you slip into this new work environment you will probably discover that new needs emerge. They might try to make themselves felt and catch your awareness through feelings of restlessness or even gloom. These feelings are trying to convey messages to you.

Pay some attention to these uncomfortable feelings and spend some time reflecting on what they are really about. Hal, for instance, has spent time contemplating the feelings of loneliness he has experienced at times since starting to work from home. 'It depends on how happy you are with yourself, and if you feel OK then the feelings of loneliness are fine,' he says. He has discovered it is all right to let yourself experience these feelings; in the process you may find that they are not a threat. They only become more difficult if they latch on to other personal, unresolved issues. Loneliness is a bit like the school bully. If it sees a weakling it latches on and makes life hell. So, for example, loneliness might latch on to your 'weak' feelings of being unwanted. As with any bullying situation, it can also be what helps a person develop as a result of having to face a very real and direct challenge.

## Lonely for What?

Although Hal feels fine about loneliness he also realizes that there are times when there is a very practical need for people in the course of his work. 'You can miss the social interaction and the ability to explore ideas, to see other people's perceptions.' This desire for professional social interaction was something which was mentioned by quite a few people whom I interviewed. Liz, for example, became concerned about how her designs were matching up to others. 'It becomes very difficult,' she says, 'to assess how one is faring. There is no feedback from other designers.'

There is the fear, and danger, while beavering away at your home base that you will become distanced from the main thinking and developments in your particular field. Because you are not working closely with other colleagues you are not so much a part of the dynamic, evolving nature of the work you do. Cross-fertilization of ideas becomes difficult; new thinking filters down more slowly to your back office; there's no one to tell you you're heading for a dead end trying to tackle a project in a particular way; other people's valuable experience ('Try this way of doing it. It worked for me last week.') is missing.

There may be a danger of blaming loneliness when really it is some other aspect of homeworking that is causing you difficulties. Instead of wailing, 'I can't bear doing this on my own any longer' and throwing in the towel, you might find on closer inspection that it is just the lack of professional input from others that is weighing you down. You are missing the input and support which only other professionals working in the same field can give you.

Next time you feel lonely, ask yourself what it is you are lonely for. Try to pinpoint it and then it will make it that much easier to keep it in perspective and to find ways of tackling it. Ask yourself whether you are lonely for:

- Approval. You might feel you need it from someone more objective than your partner or client.

- A confidence boost. Having someone say how well you are doing.
- Reassurance. You might need to know you really are doing OK.
- Any other form of professional positive stroke.
- A chat. To hear someone else's voice; to talk about something different; to share your feelings; to swap experiences; to receive a positive emotional stroke.
- Comfort. Being with other people can have a calming and relaxing effect.
- People contact. You might identify a need to feel part of life's general to-ing and fro-ing. Being in the presence of people and perhaps having a casual chat with an acquaintance, or even a stranger, might be the boost you need during the day.

You might also try to identify *when* you feel lonely. It may be that, faced with writing a difficult letter, finishing or getting started on your VAT returns or doing any number of the other activities which you personally find daunting, unpleasant or simply boring, you look round for some diversion. If you then find there is no one around or available at that moment to serve your purposes, it is easy to lapse into feelings of loneliness.

## Some Suggestions

Loneliness is a personal statement about your desire for social interaction. We're multi-faceted beings, so a solution to your own situation may involve a mix of different things to provide you with your own 'people fix':

- Cultivate your neighbours. You may find others living very close by who are having similar experiences. They might be retired, disabled, raising a young family, unemployed – or even homeworking like yourself. Gilly has found that since working at home she has become more a part of her local community. Cultivate your local shopkeepers and anyone else you see regularly.

- Structure your day so that you get the opportunity for at least a casual 'people fix'.
- If you have a computer and modem, make use of electronic mail facilities.
- Join and be an active participant in professional groups, including those for homeworkers (*see* Appendix B).
- Look closely at your own social life. You might have to work a little harder at it to make sure it gives you what you need. Simon makes this observation: 'If your social life is busy, sure you can work on your own, provided there is stimulus available at the end of your working day.'
- Assess local provisions in terms of what they can offer. If the answer is 'nothing' then you might like to consider getting some like-minded others together to change it. You might even come to the decision that you might be better off living in another area, one which is more suited to serving as a work-base.
- Keep your mind focused on your business plan. Your next step might be to find a way of building people-contact into your business. This might involve moving to shared office space, shared warehousing, or employing an assistant.
- Consider whether you could share your workspace at home with another homeworker.
- Play 'Catch the Thought'. When you find yourself saying that you feel lonely, look carefully at what has prompted the thought. It might be the prospect of completing the tax return when you'd rather be off to the pub with someone. When you do catch the thought it makes it easier to pinpoint just where the trouble lies – then you can do something about it.

- Develop a network of supporters.
- Read on to the remaining chapters.

## Deeper Problems

Finding a way to structure your new working life so that it provides you with the social and professional interaction you need will probably solve the loneliness problem. If you find that, despite taking all the positive steps you can, the feelings of loneliness persist, you may have to listen a little harder to what the feelings are telling you. Doing so on your own can be difficult, so you may want to consider finding a counsellor or therapist who can help you sort out what the underlying problems are.

Simon has eventually come to the conclusion that after working on his own at home for 10 years he has simply had enough; he is now applying for office-based jobs. He reached the point in his career where he wanted to re-evaluate what he was doing. Unhappy as a management consultant and trainer working from home, he often complained of feeling lonely. For him this prompted a radical rethink of what he was doing, how he was working and what he wanted to move on to next. There is nothing wrong with deciding that you want a change, and if you cannot find the right level of social interaction to meet your own personal needs through the work you do, even after taking active measures to redress any imbalances, then you may need to consider whether working in a self-employed capacity at home is for you.

## ▪ MOTIVATION

The other frequently mentioned bug-bear of working at home is motivation. It can come as a rather unpleasant surprise to find that as much as you may have wanted to escape from the boss telling you what you could and could not do, s/he did serve a very useful function in getting you to do anything at all. Now it's down to you – every day. And sometimes it can be hard to find the spark to get going, or keep going.

Hand in hand with motivation problems goes procrastination. When you are not motivated to do something it's easy to keep putting it off, whether it is a specific task or work *per se* – even if you turn to another useful activity instead. If you are not doing what has to be done, you are procrastinating. Cure the motivation problem and you solve the procrastination, too.

### Knowing Where to Start

A good place to start is by deciding whether something is killing off the motivation you had, or whether your motivation doesn't even seem to get off the starting-grid.

If you suspect you are becoming demotivated, reflect on what might be the culprit. Thinking back to my previous experience in an unpleasant-looking office environment, I understand that for me I can become demotivated in dreary, drab surroundings. Cast your eye around and see whether you feel your workspace might be affecting you. Inadequate lighting, uncomfortable seating or a dodgy printer might all be guilty of making the simple task of getting down to work that much harder.

On the other hand you might be the guilty one, demotivating yourself by living and breathing your work for 24 hours a day. We all need balance in our lives. You might love what you do, but if you are not taking a break from work-related activities then you are going to run the risk of losing steam. Have a look at your social activities and make sure they are up to scratch, providing you with a positive break in which to give you enough time to recharge your batteries and build that steam back up again.

## Motivating Yourself

When we are doing something we really enjoy, the work itself is the motivator; we do it because we want to do it. When we have something we don't want to do we have to find other ways of motivating ourselves. The following suggestions may help.

**Familiarize yourself again with your business plan.** It can help to remind yourself about the aims you are working towards and why you are doing what you are doing. This can help to enthuse you about the next stage you are working towards, and about how close you might be to reaching it. If necessary, keep a written reminder pinned up in front of where you work. I've got mine here, complete with my income target for the next 12 months. It's only too effective a reminder whenever I feel like putting off either work or making inroads into a project. Pin other, related reminders in all the 'distraction points' around your home. If you tend to nip off for a quick 'procrastinate' by way of the coffee pot and biscuit tin, fix copies of your bank statement, or your monthly sales targets, close by. See also Chapter 8.

You might like to think about any other **long-term motivators**. If failure to complete the work means your holiday will have to be cancelled – put up a picture of your sun-soaked destination close by. If Christmas-time would prove difficult with the bank balance in its present state, put some photos of your children by your workspace. Think about the things in your personal life you're working towards and pin up some appropriate reminders.

**Short-term reminders** might also work when you have to get yourself motivated to carry out smaller tasks. Unless you're a bookkeeper who simply loves figures, completing the VAT return is unlikely to be a motivator in itself. You will have to give yourself a different one to get yourself working on it, such as: a trip to the coffee-shop afterwards; a walk in the park; a phone-call to a friend; taking yourself out to lunch. Decide on some way to treat yourself. It might only be a small task you're having difficulties with, but if you find it doubly gruesome you might need to offer yourself a huge incentive. It's a case of 'Make it worth my while, Jack.'

**Turn your personal potential distractors into motivators.** Make deals with yourself: Half an hour's afternoon television in exchange for a two-hour period of work.

**Break the task down into manageable units.** Being faced with a monumental project can be demotivating in itself. Instead of assuming you have to complete the thing all in one go, split it into smaller sections instead, perhaps even timed sections if it's just a long, boring job like filing.

According to the deadlines you're working to, once you've broken down the task **slot it into your diary** with a start-time the following day. By doing this you're committing yourself to it. And by doing this you've already begun work on it. Give yourself a gold star. Well done!

With a whole range of things to do it is best to **draw up a list; then prioritize them.** Do the hardest one first – the rest will seem easy-peasy afterwards.

**The 'toe-dipping' approach.** Put in five minutes; that's all, just five minutes. It'll probably make you shudder, but five minutes you can stand. After five minutes see if you could possibly manage another five. If not, fine, just book another five-minute session in your diary – perhaps for the afternoon, or the next day. Keep on until the task is done.

**The dive-in-at-the-deep-end approach.** This will really make you gasp for air, but once you're in you have no choice but to spend some time in there if only while you clamber back out again. But, just like swimming (or professional paddling if you are a non-swimmer like myself) it's surprising how soon you can get used to the water – you might even find ways to enjoy it.

**Make sure you leave any ongoing task at a point where it is easy to pick up again** – your equivalent of what for me would be a half-finished sentence. Then, when you come to start again, the work is already easy to access. You don't have to hum and hah about getting into it or wondering where to start.

**Work out your own daily routine – and stick to it.** Gilly confesses that in the early days she had a definite fear of a lack of self-motivation. She overcame it by following a strict routine, aided and abetted by her family who each in turn gave her early morning calls to get her started. She now has an early-morning dog to walk, which serves the same purpose. Read on to Chapter 11.

**Farm out the tasks you really can't tolerate.** Perhaps this should only be a last resort, but it may be just the incentive you need to get you working – so that you can afford to farm them out. See Chapter 6.

**Develop a better sense of perspective.** By five o'clock this horrid job will be finished; by Thursday I'll be able to move on to something much more interesting; by next week I'll be wondering what all the fuss was about.

**Take the work to a different place.** The novelty value of doing your accounts in the art gallery might work.

**Make the task more challenging.** Give it a bit of an edge – complete it in five minutes flat; cram in six phone calls instead of two; aim to make the next sales call bring in the biggest order yet!

**Dress differently and pretend to be someone else.** Adopt the persona and act like Ms Vatman, the accountant; Mr Penne, the report-writer; Ms Selwel, the top-flight sales executive. Let them do the job instead of you.

**Don't worry!** Worry is totally ineffective. All it does is keep your mind occupied in a fretful cycle of doubt, with you rooted to the spot. However, it is a good way to procrastinate like mad.

**If appropriate, renegotiate the task with the person you're doing it for.** Improve the deadline; clarify the brief; agree a part-completion – even cancel it if you feel that awful about doing the job!

**Get some feedback.** Your lack of motivation may be linked with not getting enough feedback. Talk to your clients about how you completed the task before. Ask them if it was OK and whether they were satisfied.

**Re-evaluate.** Lack of motivation can be used as a start-point for re-evaluating your job. Your feelings may be the signal for a change of direction and an opportunity to question yourself about whether you are on the right path, heading in the right direction.

**Don't wait until you feel better about doing the task** – the only way you'll feel better is by doing it.

**If all else fails, threaten yourself with the sack!** The prospect of moving back into employment may be just the jolt you need.

You may be harbouring lots of worries and anxieties about actually getting on with the job and it may be these which are holding you back. Fear of failure is a common experience. If this applies to you, consider what positive action you might take to ameliorate these anxieties. If you feel you haven't the necessary skills then you may have to find an appropriate training course, or someone who can teach you them. One area which self-employed people can find very daunting is selling; yet selling is a skill which, like many others, can be learned with the proper training.

Thorough preparation can also help to ease anxieties. If you have a difficult phone call to make, ensure you have all the facts at your fingertips to give you more confidence.

You may also benefit from simply asking for help if your fears won't be placated. By asking for help you open yourself up to turning the situation on its head and using it as a learning experience.

Also, remember:

- Do your best – then leave it at that.
- Failing is OK – the world will still be there.
- A less-than-100 per cent performance or outcome does not mean that you are worth less than 100 per cent. Learn to separate your actions from your sense of self.
- What have you really got to lose? – especially if you understand that your actions are different from your Self.
- Go on – take a risk!

Generating your own self-motivation can be one of the biggest personal challenges when you work for yourself from home. You have domestic temptations around you all the time, from enjoying the garden to indulging in afternoon television. There will probably be times when you lose the battle, but at least you are in the position to learn from it, to heed the consequences, and also to allow yourself to slip from time to time. After all, it is your business.

## ▪ Overwork

We've talked about not being able to get on with work, but the other side of the coin is working too hard. As Alice says, 'It's very tempting simply to carry on working until all hours. One simply can't let go. Even if I watch television I work at the same time.' Basing your business at home does leave you vulnerable to overworking – just never quite managing to get completely away from it. The temptation is just upstairs, in the next room, or on the table where your papers lie. Look, they're just beckoning you over, aren't they? It can be difficult to resist and not sneak another quick look for five minutes.

When you are working for yourself there are inevitably times when you do have to burn the midnight light bulb a bit. Workflow is less easy to control in self-employment where there are times when you have to accept the work and squeeze it in, simply because you don't have anything else lined up afterwards. That's just the way it is, but it isn't really that particular situation we're talking about. Overworking or workaholism is when you find yourself so totally work-focused that there is little or no room left for anything or anyone else, including yourself. What might have started out as a habit can turn into an addiction. You know you're in trouble if you can't easily turn your mind or conversation to anything else, and if not doing work-related activities leaves you feeling uncomfortable at best, depressed or panicky at worst.

## Causes

Fear is at the root of overworking: fear of failure, which you feel you might do if you don't work the whole time; fear of losing control over what happens to your business; fear that there may be nothing left of either yourself or your life if the work were not there to fill the gap.

Overwork also seems to have pay-offs. By immersing yourself in work you can be seen to be doing something socially acceptable, and can earn other people's approval – plus some good girl/boy points. Overworking also provides you with a legitimate way in which to avoid confronting other issues in your life: emotional difficulties, family or relationship problems, personal or life issues. Putting all your hours and energies into work leaves you feeling suitably exhausted enough to justify, both to yourself and others, the fact that you are not addressing these problems. In fact, you might be so busy that you get cut off from even realizing they are there at all, leaving you to conclude you don't have any problems.

Like any addiction, being addicted to work is a way of escaping from yourself and your own reality. It may be that you are even physically addicted to the adrenalin high you get from the stressful way you work. Overworking is the same as any other drug.

## Effects

The difficulty lies in the misconception that by working longer or harder you can improve your situation. In the early days of starting up your business you will of course have had to put in a lot of effort; but that was in the early days. That same pace is not appropriate for the longer term. And because you are pushing yourself beyond healthy boundaries, effects can eventually begin to show:

- demotivation, leading to additional worry and anxieties
- mistakes, which in turn generate more work – which also costs money
- decreasing productivity

- irritability and fractiousness
- lost tempers, more often
- negative effects on relationships, including those with clients
- memory loss, leading to more mistakes and a degeneration in customer satisfaction and higher frustration levels in yourself
- more stress, as you worry about these negative effects on your business and what you can do to put it right or reclaim lost ground
- poor health as a result of the continuous adrenalin overload.

When you are really so far down the workaholic line that it becomes impossible for you to take a break from work and not feel highly uncomfortable and even distressed then you may need to find some counselling or therapeutic help to put you back on the road to recovery.

For those of you not quite as bad as this, it will help a great deal to take some time out for quiet reflection. Have a good long look at your overall lifestyle and how working at home fits into it. Just standing back from it for a moment might be enough to enable you to see where adjustments can be made. One thing which you need to do to help you break the work-focused cycle is to set yourself a realistic daily work routine – and stick to it. Reassure yourself that you can carry on with it as soon as your work day starts again tomorrow. It may be that establishing a strong buffer zone between you and your work would help. Employees achieve this by getting on a bus or train and physically leaving the work behind. When you work at home this can be more difficult. Try establishing your own switch-off routine. It might be to take a walk to the shop for an evening paper; changing clothes; pouring a drink or going out for one; putting the dinner on or collecting the children from school. You might like to experiment with a few different buffers to find out which work best for you. Read on to Chapter 8.

To help you defocus even further from work you need to establish enough interesting social and leisure activities to balance against the work you have been doing all day. More of this in Chapter 10.

## ■ OTHER DIFFICULTIES

Other personal difficulties can be encountered through working at home. What makes them perhaps more awkward is that you are on your own with them. There appears to be no one to bolster your confidence when you feel it sagging and no one to keep you from getting so blinkered that you lose all sense of perspective. Knowing that the buck stops with you and having to accept full responsibility for what goes on can be daunting and it is not unusual to doubt yourself and your abilities to handle it all from time to time. But with the right sort of support and structure to your working life, ones which suit you personally, there is no reason why your home business shouldn't go from strength to strength. Read on!

# 6 ▪ Your Essential Professional Support System

**W**hen you first start working on your business idea it is normal to focus on putting your experience and expertise to good use, and hopefully financial gain, too. Although you will have toyed with figures for the purpose of drafting your business plan, their real importance and how integral and active a part they play in your new home business may have escaped you. You will have looked at how you will bring in sales and what your marketing plan will be; the legal aspects might have been glanced at. But all in all, entrepreneurs concentrate on making their widgets or providing that quality service. After all, the other issues were dealt with in the business plan, weren't they?

It can come as a surprise to find that all those other issues play a very active and ongoing part in running your own business, and that the responsibility of handling them all is yours. This can seem quite daunting. The net result is that many procrastinate when these things do need to be addressed; others simply 'forget' about them.

This can be a difficult area for anyone who is self-employed, and possibly more so for those working at home. It may be a function of how seriously you yourself are taking your own activities. You may think, 'I don't need to sort out any tax. It's only pin-money,' or 'I've only done a few jobs,' implying to yourself that you're not a proper business person. Working in the home environment can subconsciously signal to yourself that what you are doing is not the same as someone else who is self-employed but who works in an office, shop, studio or other commercial premises. And because of this you may not feel or see the need to involve other professionals.

On the other hand, you may be the sort of entrepreneur who is only too well aware of the diverse nature of running your own show. You might be the sort who responds to this as some sort of personal challenge. The responsibility is yours and you will damn well handle it. Some believe they can and even should handle each and every aspect of their business, and that they should be sufficient unto themselves. Very noble. And I wonder how many with this attitude are also workaholics…?

## ▪ WHY USE OTHER PROFESSIONALS?

OK, so you really genuinely love playing around with figures, using your computer's accounts package. No? You cringe at the very thought of tackling those bad debtors? Whichever, think very carefully before dismissing the idea out of hand about the gains to be made by utilizing the skills of other professionals.

The normal excuse for not using outside help is money. 'I can't afford a solicitor/accountant/bookkeeper!' might be on your very lips. But let's consider another factor: your time. As an example, take the widget-maker. She's brilliant at making them, but not so good with the figure work. In fact, she finds it a real pain. 'Never was any good at maths,' she grumbles every time the books beckon. As a result, procrastination takes place. Whole days or even weeks are tainted with the worry and angst over what needs to be done. And when the task is eventually tackled it seems to take for ever. Mistakes are made; figures have to be checked again; papers and invoices don't seem to tally or get misplaced. Frustration? You bet.

All that time which has been spent trying to tackle something for which the widget-maker clearly has little ability could have best been spent making and selling more widgets! In this sort of situation, not only does the cost of your time have to be taken into account (what is your hourly rate?) but you also need to take into consideration the business which you have theoretically lost as a result. While working on the books you could have been making other sales calls – and one of them could have been *the* sale of the century! Who knows?

Nor is the answer to avoid the task. It can make the situation even worse when it is put off for prolonged periods. You could run the risk of incurring fines, penalties or interest charges; unwritten difficult letters could result in an escalation of the problem – and eventually take you even more time to sort out. Anything which needs to be done but which is put off indefinitely is very likely to lead to trouble in the long term.

Trying to do everything yourself can be costly and time-wasting. It can also affect the efficient running of your business. As a true business person you will be aiming to make your enterprise as professional and efficient as possible – won't you? Using professionals can do exactly that, and in the process make your job a lot easier and your working life simpler. Getting others to carry the burden will ease the pressure on you and provide you with more time to commit to building the business itself.

This doesn't mean that if you use outside help you are shirking your responsibilities as a business owner. Far from it. You are, in fact, acting very responsibly. Neither does it mean you can wash your hands of whichever problem you want them to handle. As the boss of your enterprise you will still have to manage the situation, only this time it will be to make sure others do the work to your satisfaction. This may be your first experience of managing someone other than yourself. It might seem unfamiliar at first, but it is an excellent skill to develop and, as your business grows, managing other people may become an important part of your job. Learning how to do so sooner rather than later gives you a head start on other competitors who might be starting up at the same time you do.

## ▪ WHICH PROFESSIONALS?

There is a core group of professionals probably worth considering for most homeworkers. Others may occur to you according to your own particular enterprise, your aims and the range of your existing skills. Here are the most common ones:

- solicitors
- accountants
- secretarial agencies
- bookkeepers
- garages
- designers

### Solicitors

The general public only encounter solicitors when they buy property or make a will. As a business person you may now want to consider the other services they offer which might help you run your business more effectively, such as helping you draw up contracts, register trademarks or take out patents; and when you start to expand they can help you with the intricacies of employment law. In general, they can help to keep you and your business on the right side of the law, making sure you don't fall foul of anything from the Trades Description Act to planning regulations.

One very important area where solicitors can be a great deal of help is with debt recovery. It's easy to end up feeling as though you are chasing your own tail rather than the debtor when you come up against poor payers. Handing the problem over to your solicitor frees you up to get on with the rest of your business.

## Accountants

Many people baulk at the prospect of using an accountant. Fear of an escalating bill, plus the assumption that the business and its turnover are too small, keep many people away. This is understandable, yet accountants can prove to be a very valuable asset to your venture. Not only do they draw up your year-end accounts, they can also advise you on the state of your business' performance and what strategies you could consider to improve the situation. And of course, they can identify areas where you can make tax savings since they know what can and cannot be offset against tax. You might even end up more in pocket by spending money on this particular professional.

As a new business, a meeting with an accountant to help you set up an easy-to-maintain and efficient accounting system can reap dividends for you. Not only will it save time and make the system easier for you to maintain, but knowing where the money is going and having efficient budgetary controls are essential if you are to keep your finger on your business' pulse and detect any signs of ill-health before drastic surgery becomes necessary.

Accountants might also be able to help you identify ways in which to help finance (or re-finance) your venture; because they are in touch with other notables they might even be able to introduce you to a backer. And when you find yourself with money of your own to invest they may be able to advise you on the best way to go about it, and even help you sort out your pension arrangements.

Accountants don't come cheap, so you need to make sure you make the best use of their professional skills. Because of this, if you really can't bear to have anything to do with figures, once you are up and running it is probably cheaper to have the weekly or monthly accounts handled by a bookkeeper, reserving the accountant for the more important tasks. See below.

## Secretarial Agencies

A one-fingered approach to typing important documents may be where you're at right now. There's nothing wrong with this, but it can be extremely time-consuming for you when you could be getting on with something which more directly could be bringing in the bucks. And despite your brave attempts, the finished article can look amateurish if you're not familiar with common layout rules. Using secretarial support to handle the more important letters, documents and other communication with clients and customers can pay dividends. A well-laid-out proposal can be a joy to read. You don't want to present something that detracts from what you are trying to say, simply because the typing and layout are so poor. It could cost you the sale.

## Bookkeepers

When you're using professional help, the main accounts, completion of tax returns and analysis of your business' financial performance should be handled by an accountant, but for the regular upkeep of your ledgers a bookkeeper is more cost-efficient. Bookkeepers do what to you might seem a drag and an absolute chore: keeping your financial records straight and balancing the books. They will deal with all those receipts you find so irksome; handle the VAT returns; deal with National Insurance and even employees' wages, if you have any. They can take the drudgery away, release you to get on with what you do best, and help keep the accountant's bill down at the end of the year by providing well-maintained accounts from which to work.

## Garages

If you depend on the use of a van or car during the course of your business, you need to have a reliable and well-maintained vehicle. Tinkering about with it might amuse you when you've a spare Sunday morning, but wrestling with a ratchet when you're trying to get to a meeting is not on. It smacks of inefficiency and can reflect on you and your business. Reliability is important. If you can't guarantee you will definitely and regularly be able to carry out the maintenance which any vehicle needs, then find a good garage or mechanic. Think of it as an investment in your business. Without your vehicle you may not be able to operate at all.

## Designers

The image your business projects can make or break it. I'm not bad with a drawing pen myself and quite enjoy drafting out ideas. But (and it's a big one), I'm *not* a professional and I recognize there are others who can do the job more effectively, more quickly and with more panache than I ever could. Designers are aware of the impact and fashion of colours, designs and typefaces. They can bring alive your ideas and help you sell them that bit more professionally.

Designers work not only on letterheads, business cards and compliment slips, they also design packaging, point of sale material, fliers, brochures and leaflets. They can give you the professional edge to take you beyond the rest of the competition, who may well be sitting at home themselves, tinkering around with their computer and a graphics package. To assume that with these two tools you can come up with designs that really add to your business image is to believe that putting a paint-brush into someone's hand will turn him or her into a Michelangelo.

Before you spend good money from your budget on something which will barely do the job, and settle for a simply typeset design chosen from a sample book at the printer's, consider investing in a designer. It could pay dividends.

## Other Professionals

If you depend on particular pieces of equipment in order to do your job, their reliability is of paramount importance. Make sure you have repairers' numbers to hand, and even consider main-tenance contracts if you haven't done so already. You may want to negotiate loan machines as part of your agreement should yours need workshop attention. You may groan at the thought of another expense, but spend a few moments considering the impact it would have if any pieces of equipment were to break down over a holiday weekend when you were trying to complete a project or order. Without the equipment you might have no business, so it's important to make sure it is looked after properly and that appropriate professional support is there as a back-up should the worst happen.

## Bank Managers

These deserve a section to themselves. Let's face it, they're important. They can be the ones to provide your business with a life-line – or take it away. It's best to try to make and maintain friendly contact with them all the way.

Probably you will be quite involved with them, and they with you, if you have taken out a business loan with them or are making use of agreed overdraft facilities on your account. But even so, I think it makes good sense to keep in friendly contact and arrange a meeting every so often, even when things are going well. Encourage them to feel involved in what you are doing, to the extent that you bring in samples, talk through your plans and share with them any particularly good news or breaks you've had. In this way they will be encouraged to give you good support when you need it because they will have a fuller understanding of what's what with your widgets. They may also be a good source of other professional contacts in your area, and may even know of people who might be interested in investing in your venture.

Bank managers aren't *all* bad.

## ▪ Choosing Your Professional

It's commonly accepted that the best way to find any professional is to ask for recommendations from people who have already been there, seen it, burnt their fingers. There is a minor caveat here in that your needs might be quite different from someone else's. Auntie Flo, who swears by her solicitor, may have only had to use him once or twice. Your case is obviously quite different: you will be looking for someone who understands the needs of a small-business person. A solicitor who handles mainly wills or divorces may hardly be the best person to help you through the legal maze of registering a trademark.

Talking to other self-employed people will perhaps give you a better idea. If you don't know of any, consider asking local shop owners, builders, decorators or anyone else who operates his or her own business in your local area. Failing that, a trip to your local Citizens Advice Bureau might help. They tend to know of local solicitors and accountants, and may be able to point you in the right direction. For other professionals – such as secretarial help and designers – local papers and the Yellow Pages will carry listings.

When you approach any professional with a view to hiring their services, you need to make sure you get the best and most appropriate person for the job. For example, not all accountants are geared towards small businesses or the self-employed. Spend some time before your preliminary meeting with them to think about what you're actually looking for. You will already have addressed the issue of where they are based, and there will be a certain amount of automatic weeding out of unsuitable others as you draw up your list of 'possibles'. Now you need to get down to the nitty-gritty: the specifics of what you are looking for; the kind of support you need; the levels of knowledge and expertise you require. Make a list of the questions you want to ask during your first meeting, and don't be afraid of asking away. If they can't give you satisfactory answers or explanations (unfamiliar terms and expressions can frequently litter these types of conversations and unintentionally confuse you), then you may well want to consider whether a good working relationship could be achieved. Withhold any decision until you've seen others for comparison's sake.

The fees they charge will be important to you. Don't be embarrassed about asking what they charge, and if you have a particular job in mind ask them for a quote, or at least an estimate. You need to know what you might be letting yourself in for financially. Solicitors and accountants can be the most difficult to pin down, since they charge by the amount of time they spend. For larger, more involved cases it can be difficult for them to assess realistically what costs might be involved until they actually start work on it, but at least get them to give you some idea. In cases like this it may be wise to agree on a financial limit which they are not to exceed without your agreement. In that way you will more easily be able to monitor the financial progress. For simpler, more straightforward cases they should be able to give you a good indication beforehand of the costs involved, say for sending a letter to someone who owes you money, or for drafting simple accounts.

Take your time in deciding whom you should use. Carefully consider all the variables together and try not to let the decision rest purely on who can give you the cheapest estimate. I've learned that lesson the hard way with plumbers. I've now found the most wonderful, professional outfit, but they're not the cheapest if you judge by looking at just the hourly rate they charge. However, they work quickly and efficiently, identifying where the problem lies and rectifying it professionally. In the long term this works out cheaper because they get the job done quickly – and I have peace of mind. That's certainly worth paying for. So look at the complete package, including (if it's important) personality and whether you feel you could work with the person or not, before committing yourself.

## ▪OTHER SORTS OF PROFESSIONAL SUPPORT

We've looked at the sort of professional support which can help you run your business more efficiently. Using them frees your home-time and may possibly even save you precious space since they will be the ones handling all the paperwork.

Another element of professional support which is important, and which many people I interviewed said they missed, was the informal support which is freely available from colleagues when you are employed. Suddenly, when you're working from home, there's no one to turn to at the next desk or down the corridor; no one to answer a simple query; no valuable, objective comments to help you along; no like-minded others to share and understand your difficulties or breakthroughs.

It's not surprising to me that this is felt so keenly. We all need to feel part of a greater whole, and this can be difficult when you're working for the most part in isolation. It's important to mix with professional colleagues, and since it is unlikely they will come crowding to Acacia Avenue to hunt you out, you are going to have to make the first move and find out where they are. They too will have felt the same as you, and may also have realized that they simply must seek out ways in which to fill this particular and important gap.

There are a number of groups and organizations that can help, including:

- your local chamber of commerce
- professional bodies
- local special interest groups
- homeworker organizations

## Chambers of Commerce

These are local forums which support and work in the interest of the local business community. They are funded in the main through membership subscriptions and can be an excellent way in which to network. For details of your local chamber, phone the Association of British Chambers of Commerce on: 0171–222 1555.

## Professional Bodies

If you have trained or are working in a specific field there may be a professional body which you could join, such as the

Institute for Personnel Management for people with a background in personnel. They can provide an excellent way in which to stay in contact with developments in your own particular field and can be an invaluable source of job-specific information.

## Local Special Interest Groups

Closer to home, you may be able to find a special business or interest group relevant to your own activities. For example, a writers' group provides me with important contact with others who understand the nature of being a self-employed writer. The strength in these groups lies in being able to provide an arena in which an interchange can take place with others working in the same field, and which can often provide you with interesting leads and contacts.

## Homeworker Organizations

Last, but by no means least, is the growing number of organizations and publications specifically for people who run their businesses from home to help us effectively network together. They address the issues which are specific to homeworkers, such as isolation, loneliness, tax arrangements and so on.

**Own Base** (*see* Appendix B for address) encourages networking and provides a regular newsletter and membership directory.

*Home Run* (0181–846 9244) is a magazine aimed at the home-based and self-employed professional.

**Telecottage Association** (0800 616008) is an organization aimed specifically at people who are teleworkers, both in an employed and self-employed capacity. Membership benefits include subscription to *Teleworker* magazine, a tele-working fact-pack, advice and support.

Not only do these groups provide you with a professional

forum and a way in which to socialize with others who share the same business interests, they may also provide you with other beneficial spin-offs: you may meet someone with whom you could possibly form a business partnership; someone who could provide the means to facilitate your business expansion and help you achieve your next business aim; someone who could provide backing; people who turn out to be the suppliers you have been looking for; someone who could become your customer of the year! Networking can have lots of benefits, not least of which is cutting through that sense of professional isolation to which homeworkers everywhere can at times be prone.

## ▪ BUSINESS ENTERPRISE ORGANIZATIONS

Besides the support afforded by the hired professionals, and the business forums, other assistance is available to homeworkers through the many enterprise organizations which have sprung up, in the main sponsored by the government. They can be a useful port of call for general information about: business practice; specific information about funding and available grants; innovation assistance; export support and advice. This is the sort of information which your accountant or bank manager may not have, and neither may the other groups you belong to who, at the very best, will only be able to provide this sort of information secondhand. It might be more time-efficient for you to go straight to the primary source – the proverbial horse's mouth.

### Training and Enterprise Councils (TEC)/Local Enterprise Companies (LEC) (Scotland)

Among other things, these organizations provide advice, help and training to people who are either thinking of going into business, or who are already there. In the majority of cases at present they will be your first port of call. They also administer the government's Enterprise Allowance Scheme. Your local TEC or LEC will be listed in the telephone directory.

## Local Enterprise Agencies (LEA)

LEAs concern themselves solely with aspects of enterprise within their specific area (as opposed to TECs and LECs, which also deal with training for non-entrepreneurs). They are sometimes subcontracted by the local TEC or LEC to carry out their enterprise function. For your nearest LEA, contact Business in the Community: 0171–629 1600.

## Business Links

Realizing that it can be very confusing to find your way around the maze of different agencies, a network of One-Stop Shops is being set up in England (Wales and Scotland are developing their own models). Their aim is that by the end of 1995 every business will have access to a Business Link – a partnership between Enterprise Agencies, Chambers of Commerce and other diverse, business-support organizations which will, in the end, make it that much easier for you to access the information you want. For details of your local provision, phone Business Links: 0114 – 259 7507.

## Prince's Youth Business Trust

Help is offered through the Trust to young entrepreneurs in the form of grants and ongoing training (0171–321 6500).

## Livewire

A similar scheme, sponsored by Shell to help young entrepreneurs make a successful start in self-employment (0191–261 5584).

## Federation of Small Businesses

This is a lobbying organization, working in the interests of people who are self-employed or running small businesses. Membership provides you with a regular newsletter and access to professional advice (01253 720911).

## Regional Development Agencies

Some areas have specific needs, and because of this Regional Development Agencies have been set up to encourage and attract businesses to help regenerate them. For details of what additional support might be available in your area, contact your local TEC or LEC in the first instance.

## Economic Development Unit (EDU)

Each town hall has an EDU which monitors business activity within its area. They too can be a useful pointer to grassroots business support provision and local forums. They can also help you with relevant statistics when drawing up business plans, for example about the age of the local population, ethnic mix, and so on.

## Business Resource Centres

Your local council may run a Business Resource Centre. Not only do they provide local and easily accessible business information and support, they also have computers, fax and copying machines among their support facilities for small-business people to use.

## Business Debtline

Should you find yourself in financial deep water, contact the Business Debtline. They provide an advisory service on managing and getting out of business debt. Phone them for a self-help pack: 0121–236 0595.

## ▪ POLITICALLY AFFILIATED ASSOCIATIONS

If you are a member of a political party, check whether they have a small-business support off-shoot. By joining them you know they will be working in sympathy with your own political leanings, and they may offer a range of additional benefits such as insurance discounts.

Professional and personal isolation can be very difficult to manage and a sense of it can strike the surest home-based worker. Most of us experience it at some time or other; it's one of the hazards of the job. However, by building into your working life a network of professional support you can minimize the risk of suffering from a decline into terminal isolation, and in the process maximize the efficiency of your own business.

If some of the suggestions are really not financially viable at the moment, use them as targets and build stages into your business plan to help you get there. It is a sign of strength to make full use of professional advice, drawing on the best available to help ensure that you and your business succeed.

# 7 ▪ Making Use of Helping Hands

We've had a look at the important part which using professional support can play in the working lives of homeworkers. It can make a great deal of difference to how successfully you manage your business, as well as to your own sense of well-being. But there is also another resource which you could be making use of and which is closer to hand: that which is afforded by your family and friends.

I can almost hear the shrieks and wails from some homeworkers who primarily see these people as irritants during the working day, only too keen to interrupt at the slightest opportunity – which is inevitably when you could least do with it. We'll have a look at some of these difficulties more closely in Chapter 9, but in the meantime it may be worth while to consider what they might have to offer which you could be putting to good use.

## ▪ INDEPENDENCE

The prospect of turning to others may bring you up against some deeply entrenched personal beliefs about yourself. Independence might be the one word you'd choose for your work-based coat of arms. It sums up how you feel about being strong, coping, doing it yourself, managing. I used to relate to this word, some might say almost fiercely, and woe betide anyone who threatened it. 'I can do it, thank you.' 'I can manage,' were frequently on my lips as I grappled with an irksome problem. But at least I wasn't being dependent on someone else, I thought. It seemed to me, and it might to you, too, that you can only be either dependent or independent. Then someone pointed out to me the word *interdependent*. Hadn't heard that one before. It stumped me. I couldn't argue a retort because it didn't instantly seem to challenge my precious independence.

Being totally dependent on someone or a group of 'someones' is of course unhealthy. It prevents you from facing up to and meeting those challenges which may be well within your capabilities and which would extend your present range of skills and experience. It is only through doing so that we grow. Apart from cutting you off from your chance to develop it also leaves you in a very vulnerable position. What happens if that person disappears or lets you down? If you have become too dependent it could really throw a spanner in the works.

If the prospect sends you scurrying rapidly to the other end of the scale, i.e. towards total independence, that too can leave you vulnerable – and isolated. You've put up the barriers; no helping hand is allowed in. But then once people get the message and stop offering, the quietness after the clamour can seem odd. Looking up and around you see that everyone has indeed got the message and cleared off, obligingly doing what you said you wanted them to do. They have left you alone. No one is there. Now you realize how vulnerable a position you've put yourself in. You've cut yourself off from any assistance at all; assistance which you could really do with right now.

Neither extreme seems helpful and neither puts you in a strong position. What *would* is to put interdependence into practice instead. It made me smile when it was pointed out to me that although I professed to be totally independent I still took my shoes to someone else to have them repaired. No, I had to admit that by doing so I did not feel that my independence was under threat. I go to restaurants where other people not only cook the food but clear away afterwards for me as well. Nope. No threat there either. The point started to hit home that we are all very much interdependent in numerous ways, and none of them threatens anyone's independence. In fact, having someone else do things like sweep the streets outside and remove the refuse from my dustbin actually gives me greater freedom and releases me from being tied to all the worries and concerns about what I am going to do with a bin full of rubbish or a street full of litter.

Interdependence is OK. It doesn't rob you of your independence, neither does it make you a dependent weakling. It offers you the chance to manage your life more effectively and efficiently by drawing on and using resources which are available to you. Far from taking anything away, being interdependent gives you more freedom.

If you're still not convinced, reflect on the fact that you're reading a self-help book.

## ▪ WHAT SUPPORT DO I NEED?

Before you can start asking for and making use of any sort of informal support, it's useful if you first spend some time thinking about what you need:

- to feel less over-burdened?
- to have more free time to yourself?
- to have more time with friends and family?
- to be able to get out of the house more often?
- to get some input for yourself (because you are putting so much of yourself into your business)?
- to be more focused on the real nub of your work?

- to connect more with people?

Carry on thinking about your work and any discomforts which arise during the working day – possibly afterwards, too (although we'll be having a look at the home front in Chapter 9). If it's hard to think of anything right now, continue with this exercise throughout your next working day or two and jot down things as they come up.

Next make a list of what help you would like in an ideal situation. Don't censor anything. Write it all down, regardless of whether you think you could get the help right now or not. Use the list to prompt you into action. Here's a list that might give you a helping hand in getting started:

- Think about your emotional needs, which you might feel are not being met, and how you would like them fulfilled.
- Think about any tasks in your job which you find tedious and which you would love not to have to do.
- What do you consider peripheral to your real work yet which still has to be done?
- What specific work situations do you find difficult to handle, either task- or people-wise?

Carry on with your list, making it as specific as you can.

From starting off believing you can manage on your own, or that you *are* managing on your own, you might be a little surprised to find that there are quite a few areas where a helping hand wouldn't go amiss. And it hasn't made you weaker by one iota! Learning about your own needs allows you to work out the best way to see that you receive the necessary support. This is the ultimate in acting responsibly.

Now that you can see the shortfalls, the nature of the beastie becomes apparent, making it easier to decide what can be done.

## ■ WHO COULD HELP?

Perhaps first we need to establish whose hands could come in most useful. Try to avoid the temptation of thinking no further than your partner or best friend. No one person can provide you with all the different types and levels of support you need, nor should anyone be expected to. It seems to me that this could lead only too quickly to Resentment Time. Instead, your list can include the names of many others, your partner being just one of them:

- immediate family members (including children)
- aunts, uncles, grandparents and more distant family members
- friends
- ex-work colleagues
- neighbours
- contacts made at church or other place of worship
- contacts made through other groups to which you belong
- other casual acquaintances such as shopkeepers and the chap you meet in the pub now and again.

Think long and hard about whom you know, not only those in your intimate circle but also those with whom you perhaps only occasionally chat.

## ■ WHAT MIGHT BE ON OFFER?

Now you can inventory what each person might have to offer. For some the answer will be obvious; for others you may draw only a blank right now (and for these at least you now have a conversational starting-point for the next time you meet!) If you're looking for someone who can give you some good objective advice about choosing a solicitor, you may find out what that woman you are friendly with at the gym knows. You may have to dig around to find what you need in the right person.

With a more complete list the next task is to do a mix and match. Link up the needs and wants you have with the skills, experience and abilities of those you know. Even seven-year-old Sam could help by sorting out your desk-tidy for you or posting letters. Look at the whole range of possibilities and map out how you might usefully be able to integrate their help into your business activities. Auntie Flo who lives 200 miles away may appear to have little to offer, but think about how she might be able to assist you in getting press releases to the right person on her local papers and also help you expand your sales activities in her locality. She might also be able to give you some ideas about expanding your range of goods or services to include something for her age or interest group.

The more practical ways of how people might be able to help may be relatively obvious, since it is quite a simple task to find out whether someone is any good at typing. The benefits to you are therefore going to be easy to gauge. But there are other, less obvious ways in which friends and acquaintances can help you along the way.

## ▪ EMOTIONAL SUPPORT

One important way in which they can help is by giving you emotional support. It's very hard setting up any new enterprise, and running one in isolation at home while it feels as if the rest of the world is having some sort of giant party at the office can make it feel even harder at times. On top of this, until you've built up a strong network of professional and non-professional support-givers you will be carrying the burden of each and every aspect of your business alone. Add to this the stress of wondering whether the customers are going to appear, and when they do whether they will ever come back again. On a bad day doubts can assail you at every turn, and even on a good day there can be some pretty stressful moments even if it's only because you've realized you haven't spoken to anyone more intelligent than the newsreader on the television – and that's worrying!

This is where those significant others can step in and fill the breach. Let's have a run-through of what they might be able to offer:

- They can encourage you when you feel as though you might fail.
- They can bolster your confidence when it starts to seep away.
- They can help you keep a sense of perspective, reminding you of your successes when all you can see is gloom.
- They can listen to you while you pour out your worries, concerns and anxieties.
- They can make it seem all right again.
- They can provide a shoulder to cry on.
- They can be a positive distraction to take your mind off work and get you out of the hamster-in-a-wheel mode.
- Being with others, and not even talking about work, can reduce stress levels.
- They can be challenging, in a positive way.
- They can help you celebrate when times are good and share with you in your successes.
- It can be a real tonic to listen to others and let them provide you with different topics of conversation, news items and a new range of ideas.

## *They Can Do All That?*

They can if you help them. I don't mean you have to barter to get them to give you the emotional or practical support you need. I mean that you have to be the enabler, the facilitator. You have to help them to help you; not always, but some of the time.

At the moment you've only thought about and listed the help you would like. The next step is to plan how you might go about getting that help. We're talking here about communication; a skill which many people have yet to cultivate successfully. That's why we all experience so many misunderstandings and difficulties with people. What we intend to say can often come out very differently, and also the way we say something can be interpreted differently again by the people we're talking to. As they open their mouths to reply we start the cycle of misunderstanding again. I frequently wonder that we ever succeed with anything more basic than a smile. At times it can seem as though our spoken words take on a life of their own.

The only thing you can do is to **prepare well** before you open your mouth. Be clear with yourself about what you want to ask for. A garbled 'I could do with some help around here,' is too vague for anyone to respond to in any intelligent, or helpful, manner. Here are some guidelines which you might find helpful in formulating your requests for help:

- Be very clear about the help you are asking for and the length of time which may be involved in a task.
- Work out any payment you might need to offer.
- Carefully choose your moment to speak.
- Avoid the Uriah Heep stance of being 'orribly 'umble.
- Get straight to the point – avoid prevaricating.
- Be prepared for a 'No', but avoid assuming beforehand that this will be the outcome. If you expect to be knocked back this will come across as soon as you open your mouth (possibly

before then), through your body and facial gestures. The unspoken message 'You won't be able or want to help,' will be picked up by the person you are talking to and possibly prime him or her to oblige by turning your request down.

- Let the person answer you fully before you speak again. Avoid jumping in straight away and saying something like 'I know. You can't help. I shouldn't have asked. Forget it.' Give the other person a chance.

- If the person does refuse, make sure you understand whether this means he can't help just now, or that he might be able to later.

- Check whether the person can help in any other way; is she willing to be asked again some other time? Does she know of anyone else who might help?

- If you are refused remember that the other person is refusing the request – not you. He is giving an honest reply to a question you've asked. He's not rejecting you.

Asking for help doesn't come easily or naturally to all of us. You might have to give it some practice. What will help is asking in an assertive manner, devoid of embarrassment or other emotions likely to elicit the sort of response you do not want. Once you have the question clear in your mind, practise saying it openly, directly and calmly. There's no need to gabble on afterwards with justification after justification. Leave the question there for the other person to respond to. This works with requests for both practical and emotional support.

Being open and direct about what you would like avoids the many confusions which can come about from people feeling their goodwill is being abused or that they are being manipulated in some way. For example, if you have had a lousy day and really need to sound off about it, check with your partner first: 'I've had such a lousy day. I'd really like to let rip about it for 10 minutes. Is that OK?' By asking they can see you're not taking them for granted; it gives them the option to say no (they might need a cup of tea first); they might have had a worse day than yours and will feel resentful if they have to listen to you unburden first. If they say 'Yes' then you won't be plagued by wondering whether they really want to listen or not.

You might also like to consider stressing what you want out of such exchanges. We rarely want people to be solving our problems for us or telling us what we should or should not do. Explain beforehand that all you want is an ear, and perhaps a cup of tea to go with it. A sympathetic listener can do wonders, and by making it clear that others understand you're not expecting them to provide any answers, they will feel happier about giving you both of their ears without feeling threatened by the prospect of being over-burdened.

Practise asking questions assertively. It will be enormously beneficial in helping you to get the help you want. When people understand exactly what it is you're asking for they are more able to give you an honest and direct response, thus avoiding time-consuming and energy-draining misunderstandings and resentments on either side.

## ▪ MANAGING THE HELPERS

With the practical help you receive, you might find you come up against the difficulty of managing other people's workmanship. It's a problem which a lot of people who start to delegate can encounter. You expect someone to perform the task in exactly the same way you would, and to the same standard. What a shock to find that others do things differently!

If it is really crucial how something is done and that a standard be observed, then be clear with the instructions you give.

Stand by and make sure they have understood what you meant, and that they can satisfactorily demonstrate their understanding to you. Packing items carefully which could otherwise get damaged does need to be done to a certain standard, so it's down to you to make sure they understand what is expected of them. Once you're satisfied that they can do it as you require, let them get on with it.

Depending on the nature of the help, you might have to accept that things can be done differently from the way you would choose to do them. So long as this doesn't topple your enterprise then learn to live with it. Who knows, you might even pick up a few tips and discover that their way is even better than yours.

## ■ SUPPORT GROUPS

Despite the practical and emotional help afforded by the people you know, you may still feel that there are gaps left. You may find you need other like-minded self-employed people to call upon, or people who do similar work to yourself, yet perhaps the professional organizations and groups you might join are too remote or do not operate at such a grassroots level. Also, Auntie Flo might be a wonderfully sympathetic listener but sometimes you really do need to ask a fellow professional how she would deal with a specific matter and what experience she might be able to bring to bear on a problem.

To remedy the situation you might consider getting a few other kindred spirits together to form your own support group. If you are feeling the need for this kind of arrangement where you live, then there are probably others who also feel the same.

It needn't be a grand or complex affair; in fact the simpler the better for a support group. Think in terms of around five to eight people, although finding even one other might be sufficient. Very large groups can be difficult to manage effectively, and finding suitable meeting places can be awkward.

There's no need to make it terribly formal with a whole creed about how it should operate, membership rules and so on. The simple aim is to provide a meeting place where mutual support can be offered. Monitor the development of the group and review its success, then you can decide together on its future direction and aims.

Although professional help and support is vital to ensure you get the most out of yourself and the best for your business, the informal support which friends, family and acquaintances might offer can be invaluable. Your accountant can explain how you might reduce your overheads and increase profits, but just as important is receiving the emotional and practical support you need closer to hand.

It might not come easy to all of us to ask for, and even receive help, but by doing so and utilizing our interdependence we can discover for ourselves a new freedom which allows us to take ourselves and our home businesses to greater heights of success. As Hal says of his support network, 'They're pretty important. Not that I couldn't survive without them but I think my sense of well-being would be impoverished. I think you need both positive strokes and criticisms to develop both professionally and as a person.'

# 8 ▪ Helping Yourself Along

F inding and using the support of other people can prove to be a real boon, giving you that extra boost we all need from time to time when we're working from home. But perhaps the support that is most difficult to access is that which we can provide ourselves. It's easy to look elsewhere for ways to solve our problems, but sometimes the problems can actually be ourselves. Our working practices can positively militate against our effectiveness, and this can happen only too easily when we're working in the relaxed atmosphere of our homes.

In this chapter we will have a look at ways in which we can stop sabotaging and start enabling ourselves in our work. The tools at our disposal are *goals*, *time management* and *problem solving*.

## ▪ VISION

Every successful entrepreneur and business executive I know of cites one vital element for achieving success: having a vision. We all need to know where we're heading if we're ever going to get there. Otherwise even Dorothy in the *Wizard of Oz* would have ended up wandering around for ever and would never have found the Emerald City. How could she if she didn't know that was where she was heading? She wouldn't even have known to start on the yellow brick road. Similarly, without a vision none of us can effectively set off on our own journey.

You may have already clarified your aims in drawing up a

business plan. If not, do spend some time working out what yours really are. It might be no more ambitious than earning enough to keep the cat in sardines, or it might be to overtake McDonald's as market leader. Whatever your aim and ambition it will affect the rest of your business life and will be the driving force behind your actions and decisions; the thing that keeps you motivated. Because it is so important you need to feel 100 per cent committed to your aim. Your energy needs to be all there behind it. You must really believe in and want to reach your goal.

Having said that, also bear in mind those goals which belong to your personal life. You don't want to be so single-minded that you override and ignore them. A successful business will be cold comfort if your personal and family life has fallen apart in the meantime. You're aiming for a balance in your life between your home business and what you want it to achieve, and your home and social life.

We need to have our aims worked out and placed securely in our minds, ready to refresh us on those grey mid-winter after-noons; using them to remind us why we are here, and helping us to avoid the danger of having everything lose its meaning, leaving us demotivated and possibly not wanting to go on.

## Objectives

So, you know where you and your business are heading, in a general sort of way. You've pointed your finger to the wide horizon; but it's still a little hazy over there. How will you know you've reached where you thought you were going without a better description of your destination?

Objectives are used to firm up that vision. Yours might see you as head of a successful widget-making business, in which case your objectives will specify that you will:

- get there in the next 10 years
- be the market leader
- have six operations distributing worldwide, in the US, UK, Canada, Russia, Australia and South Africa
- have a yearly turnover of £2 billion.

Now that's pretty specific, and if you were serious about this you would obviously go into lots more detail. Objectives take away the woolliness of aims. They have a time element and are measurable, that is, at the end of the time-limit you will be able to judge if you have reached your aim. Without the objectives you might still be wondering when you retire whether you 'made it' or not.

Look again at your vision and clarify it with objectives to bring it sharply into focus. Think about time-scales, turnovers, number of employees, number of outlets and any other measurable element which is relevant to your own operation regardless of how small or big you eventually want it to be. Flesh out that vision until it becomes crystal-clear.

## ■ GOALS

So now you're really clear about where you're heading. But to launch into work on Monday morning with nothing more than The Grand Plan can be a bit daunting. After all, you know it's going to be 10 years before you get there, and right now that seems an awful long way away and your legs aren't long enough to take you there in one wild leap.

The next challenge is to work out how you are going to get there. The tools to use are goals. These are more bite-sized than aims, which tend to be all-encompassing but don't really tell you much about how to get there. They merely beckon.

Goals are the stopping-off points along the road, eventually leading you to your own Emerald City. They mark the route and lead you in easy stages to where you want to be. They help make the situation more manageable, the journey more tolerable.

You need to think about what your long-term goals are; the longest one already being worked out. Think about your goals for the next 10 and 5 years. From there it will become easier to see what you need to do this year to set you firmly on the road and help you set your focus. Once you've established your long-term goals, year by year, pin them up near your workplace. Mine are just behind my computer; any lapses are quickly shaken off by a quick glimpse at these figures.

A year is still quite a hefty chunk of time, so next think about monthly goals and the points you need to reach throughout the year to keep you on target. When you have done this you will end up with your plan for the coming 12 months.

And so it filters down until you're working out what you need to do this week, and what you need to do today; the *today* goals being the real nitty-gritty. Having spent this time thinking about where you really want to be heading, you might even change your attitude to what you previously had intended to do today. Being aware of your goals enables you to judge the usefulness of any activity – and also of any diversions which occur. If it doesn't help you take another step towards your vision then perhaps it isn't useful at all. But remember, although goals should be challenging they should also be realistic. They are a guide rather than a stick to beat yourself with. Neither should they be rigid; times change and so do you, so build in regular reviews to check whether your goals are still realistic, and also whether you still want to achieve them or not.

## Benefits of Goal-setting

The benefits of setting both short- and long-term goals are:

- They enable you to manage yourself and your time better.
- They enable you to be pro-active, not reactive.
- Goal-setting improves productivity.
- They help you see where and how you can effectively build support into your working life.
- They enable you to maintain a balance between your work and personal life.
- They enable you to develop ways of working and living which are beneficial to your health and well-being.

Whenever you reach one of your goals, acknowledge it and reward yourself. If it's a major goal then bring out the big celebratory guns; if it's a small one give yourself half an hour in the sunshine. And if you fail to reach any goal, acknowledge that too so that you can more easily let the sense of failure go. If it has been a ghastly day when nothing has gone right, then acknowledge it just as you would a reward, so that it doesn't drag around after you. Perform some activity to put a full-stop after any failure, like taking a shower or going for a walk.

Goals are such an important way in which to help yourself along. Working at home can be very hard, and momentum difficult to maintain; by keeping long-term goals in sight and setting short-term, attainable yet challenging goals you run a better chance of keeping that momentum and important motivation going.

## ▪TIME MANAGEMENT

Although you may now have your goals set and know where you are going, managing your time to ensure you achieve those goals can still present problems. As an employee there is always someone to answer to and account for your time. Deadlines are handed out and a boss is always there to make sure you aren't slacking. When you're at home there's only yourself to keep you on the straight and narrow – which is now wide and very comfortable, thank you very much. Perhaps a bit too comfortable?

We need to employ every tactic at our disposal to make sure we can enjoy the great range of advantages which working at home offers, while minimizing the disadvantages which working alone in such a comfortable environment can bring.

Time management is often described as a way of giving you control over your time. By working at home you already have control and are exercising it. Spend a moment to consider the extent and quality of your own personal control. You may realize it could do with a bit of improvement.

Improving your time management enables you to manage the peaks and troughs which are a part of being self-employed. Sometimes there is a glut of work and next week a dearth. With better time management you will more easily be able to handle these fluctuations, and even minimize them. For example, by building a regular time into your weekly schedule, say a day or so, dedicated to marketing and lining up your next customer you should be able to reduce the likelihood of gaps between each project or order while you find the next client. Gaps are costly. So are other aspects of poor time management: think how much extra you are charged by printers to do a rush job, simply because you let time slip by before you got around to dealing with it. Think also about how rushed you feel having to handle situations like that. There's not only the financial cost to bear in mind, but also the cost to yourself in terms of additional stress.

Good time management is important to anyone who works for him- or herself. Your costings will depend on how much time it takes to complete orders or fulfil contracts for customers. Without using your time effectively, or even knowing how much time you spend on different activities, you run the risk of under-charging, not covering your costs, and reducing your profitability. As a result of managing your time better you may be able to:

- reduce your costs
- bring in more work
- review your pricing, and possibly increase it – or increase certain aspects of it
- pinpoint any aspects of your work which might be totally unprofitable
- reduce your stress levels
- save money.

## Starting Here

Before looking at specific time-management measures, it's best to know what point you're starting from. Everyone has different work practices and schedules, with many of us falling into a haphazard pattern of responding to what presents itself as needing to be done. Crisis management is perhaps too strong a term for it, but this may in essence be how you are operating.

In order to know which point you are starting from, keep a time diary for a few days (a week if possible). Note down when you start and finish each activity, including responding to interruptions, phone calls and rest breaks. Note whether interruptions are work-related, personal and welcome, or personal and unwelcome. Note too your emotional reactions and response times. A two-second episode might provoke a half-hour emotional reaction. Also make a note of changes in your energy and concentration levels throughout the day. Identify when they peak and also when they seem to hit any low points.

By seeing what sort of patterns you work to at present, you will be able to recognize more easily where improvements could be made. It's not unusual for people to find that their perception of how they work is far different from the reality, and in some cases the only pattern which can be identified is that there is no pattern at all. This is not to say that working in such a way automatically means an inefficient or ineffective use of time, but informal work patterns do need to be looked at carefully to assess the impact they might be having on your business and its efficiency. We all have our own ways of working and what might appear to be chaotic to others might be best for your energy and flow of concentration.

## Organizing Yourself

Another thing to check before you can look into specific ways in which to improve your time management is your basic level of organization. Some management writers say that working tidily at your desk is essential. When I'm in full flow on a project, I know my workspace is anything but. Yet that is how I carry out my work, and I can't see any way to get around having spreads of papers and piles of books. Being tidy for the sake of it seems to me to be another way of creating more work. However, I do agree that organizing your basic workspace and back-up facilities is important. Here are a few tips:

- Make sure you are getting the best out of the facilities you use, including suppliers, other people, computer programmes and space.

- Like me, the way you work may appear untidy, but make sure you have the materials you need and the space you work at organized so that you know where everything is.
- Pin-boards, shelves, waste-bins, desk tidies, drawer tidies and in/out trays are all simple, cheap and effective ways to organize your workspace and help you work efficiently.
- Make sure your address books and indexes are up to date, and your reference materials close to hand.
- Find a large attractive dish to use as a dump for keys, credit cards, money, etc. Then you'll always know where to find them.
- A workable filing system is incredibly important. An inefficient one costs you time and money. If you can't quite get your head round this one, find someone with secretarial skills who might be able to help you sort out a good system.

## Time-Management Helpers

Here is a list of time-management tricks, suggestions and points for you to consider:

- Time-table regular chores into your diary. Because they are routine they can often be ignored when it comes to allotting them the necessary time, leading to frustration, resentment and errors when you do get round to tackling them – a real waste of valuable time and energy.
- Be realistic about how much time it takes to do the 'five-minute' chore. From beginning to end it may take more like half an hour.
- Build breaks into your time schedule and write them into your diary. They're your appointments with yourself.
- Using information from the time-diary you keep, allow for

interruptions, perhaps by adding 5 or 10 minutes to the estimate for each task.

- List what needs to be done each day. I prefer to do this at the end of the previous day to make use of my dwindling energy and to help me wind down from work. It also provides the opportunity to put into action anything that's needed for the following day, such as sending a fax.
- In drawing up your To Do List:
  - Prioritize what you have to do.
  - Don't include anything more than you know you can realistically achieve; there's always the next day.
  - Put in one or two really easy tasks at the top of your list to help you get started.
  - Set a realistic time schedule.
  - Include time-gaps in between appointments, for travel or simply to give you time to clear away from one and prepare for the next.
  - Don't forget to include any family or social obligations which might affect your working day.
- Always evaluate what you *think* you have to do. Ask yourself if each task is really necessary; whether it could be delegated; whether it could be subsumed into another task; whether you could junk it.
- Plan meetings carefully: stick to the agenda and make sure you finish in the time allocated.
- Include in your daily routine a buffer – some activity that serves to mark the separation of work from home at the beginning and end of every day. It could be a walk to the shops, changing your clothes, or some other simple ritual. I end my working day with the early evening television news.
- Despite modern technology, time-consuming paper can still clog up the works. The rule of thumb is that you should handle each piece of paper only once. Read it and then either

file it, bin it or act on it – either straight away or by noting in your diary when you will deal with it if it involves a more complex issue.

- Keep a large scratch pad to hand for jotting down thoughts, things you've remembered you need to do, ideas and so on. Making a quick note saves you from having to interrupt your present workflow in order to take action straight away. It enables you to complete the task in hand without interrupting yourself.

- Learn your limits and what you can comfortably handle, then – instead of trying to do lots of things and not doing any of them particularly well – you will be able to achieve better results on the things you do work at. You're not Superwo/man.

- Use a kitchen timer to save you having to clock-watch until you reach the end of an allotted time period for a specific task. Set it for 30 minutes if that is how long you plan to work on your accounts. I find external reminders like this more effective at signalling when to end a piece of work than the messages I try to give myself in my head.

- Practise saying 'No'. Delivering necessary refusals is one of the best ways of making sure you keep focused and on track. To help you:
  - Develop some useful stock replies for common requests and interruptions.
  - Direct is best: 'No, I can't right now,' is better than 'Well, erm, really I, erm . . .'
  - Don't justify your answer; it provides the other person with an opportunity to find a way around your refusal. Instead, be pro-active and suggest an alternative which is more convenient for you.
  - Point the person making the query in the direction of someone else who might be able to help.

- • If you find you've agreed to something and then wish you hadn't, phone back and cancel; something has to take priority and it should be you and your business. If you find this difficult, remember you're turning down the request, not the person.
- Specific situations which always take their toll on you emotionally for extended periods of time (complaints from customers; refusals from potential clients; minor frustrations which seem to send you into a towering rage) signal underlying issues that need to be addressed, primarily for the sake of your well-being but also to avoid the continual waste of valuable time. Read on to Chapter 12.
- Let others know your schedule. It will not only help them understand why and when you're not available, but also help to make your intention concrete.

Having said all this, I do believe it is important to know yourself and work with your own time-style. Listen to your own voice and raise your awareness about whether you are being as effective as you can be. The way you work is only a problem if it affects your efficiency, or if it generates or masks negative feelings within yourself such as unhappiness, dissatisfaction or guilt.

Experiment with new ways of working, with new routines. Only you will know what works best for you. Day-dreaming might seem like an appalling waste of time to others, but for you it might be the way your inner wisdom signals that you need a brief rest, creative time-out, time to digest information or to allow you intuitively to work through a problem.

Also bear in mind your own particular body-clock. It's pointless trying to schedule taxing tasks for nine in the morning when you don't really get going until eleven. Work with your Self, and find ways of scheduling your day so that your best comes through.

## *Be Strategic and Selective*

By developing and using your own particular mix and match of time-management techniques which maximize your resources rather than squander them, you can be more selective – and therefore more strategic – about what you do. You can judge how well or not activities fit into your overall plan by:

- deciding which tasks can easily be delegated to either paid or unpaid others
- evaluating the importance of a task, rather than making knee-jerk reactions about it
- eliminating unnecessary tasks
- evaluating whether there's a better way of handling a task
- asking 'Does it serve a purpose?' and 'Does it serve my purpose?'
- asking 'Does it help me move towards my goal?'
- deciding whether it could be done later.

Finally, to put you on your way to improving your time-management techniques, put a date and time in your diary when you will start to review/employ/tackle some of your own time-management issues. Do it now!

## ▪ PROBLEM SOLVING

With effective planning and time management you may find that some difficulties and problems resolve themselves. But problems are part of life, and even if some of them have faded away with your new schedules and planning techniques there will always be more problems and challenges waiting their turn.

Adopting the ostrich approach and ignoring them in the hopes that they'll go away rarely works. Not realizing that you're ignoring them on purpose, problems think you can't see them so they grow bigger and bigger, and eventually start shouting at you.

Problems have an awful lot of energy in them just bursting to be released, so unfortunately the sticking-plaster approach to solving them does not really work either. Since they haven't been dealt with, they again think you've simply forgotten them and eventually start getting restless. Then, ping! Off shoots the sticking plaster to reveal the festering mess beneath.

Like it or not, problems need to be dealt with and, as they say, the sooner the better.

## Tackling Problems

First of all, it is important to make sure you really understand the nature of the problem. If you misdiagnose it then you're more likely to choose the wrong treatment, so really scrutinize it well. Not having a car might appear to be the problem, but on closer inspection the real underlying issue is about getting goods from a supplier to you, or from you to a customer, which in fact offers more solutions than just the one which involves you and your transport. Looking at the underlying issues opens up a whole range of other solutions. Always look at the underlying causes beneath what you initially define as the problem.

Also, assess whether the problem is a one-off or part of an ongoing pattern, and whether it is likely to occur again. This will affect your decision about which solution is most appropriate. A longer-term strategy than you first envisaged may be what is called for.

Then:

- Jot down immediate possible solutions.
- If necessary get others to help by running a brainstorming

session – that is, describe the problem and invite suggestions; write *all* of them down (*don't* pre-judge any of them – not even by smiling or making a flip comment about it; this can inhibit the creative process). Analyse the suggestions afterwards.

- List the pros and cons of each suggestion, keeping in mind your overall aims and objectives and any possible effects on your time.
- Choose from the results.
- Another method is to ask the question out loud to yourself and then go and do something else. Take your mind off the problem entirely and leave it alone for a while to give your subconscious time to work on it. Importantly, when you use this method keep a note pad to hand at all times; you'll probably find the answer popping into your head at the most unexpected moment – be warned.
- From here, develop your plan of action, if necessary breaking it down into smaller steps.
- Allocate time for necessary action in your diary, including any preparation time.
- Also allocate time to review the outcome. Has the solution been successful, achieved your aims, solved the problem?
- If it has not been a success, see what needs to be changed and use an opportunity for learning and developing. Remember, it only means the solution hasn't worked, not that you're a failure.
- If it has worked, celebrate and reward yourself and anyone else who has been involved.

Get the feel of the different tools you have at your command to help yourself along. Develop the models which you like best and with which you feel you can most easily work. Hopefully they will help make the difficulties which can assail all home-workers more easy to cope with.

# 9 ▪ On the Home Front

Although it can be very demanding setting up a business, becoming self-employed and establishing a workspace at home, these practicalities can pale in comparison with the difficulties that you can encounter with your nearest and dearest.

The aim in running your business from home is that everyone benefits and no one loses out. What a challenge! Unfortunately it is only too easy for the situation to fall out of balance, with either work taking over your home and family life, or vice versa. Neither is healthy and both should be avoided. In this chapter we'll have a look at some suggestions as to how that delicate balance might be achieved and, just as importantly, maintained.

## ▪ SIMON'S EXPERIENCE

Because both you and your work are in the family or shared domestic domain, how everyone feels and reacts to the new set-up is a crucial element of your business' development and success. People's emotions are delicate yet potentially volatile things needing skilful and patient handling, otherwise the situation can only too easily turn sour, as Simon found out. This is what happened to him:

*When the long-term contract I had came to an end I decided I wanted to make money and be self-employed. My wife wasn't ecstatic; you couldn't say she was over-pleased because of the irregular income and insecure future. She wanted to leave London and my self-employment decision meant the move had to be put off indefinitely. I wanted to go self-employed regardless of what she thought. She, on the other hand, was very security-minded.*

*So right from the start there was an element of conflict and I didn't feel I had much support. It was awful: she'd knock on my door and say 'I'm off to the shops. Look after the children' (a baby and a three year old). It was very disruptive for my work-pattern and I felt set up. There were always minor interruptions. We never agreed a way around them. We'd have words but then she'd do the same thing again. She wanted company but I was busy. She just couldn't appreciate I was at work, just as surely as if I were 20 miles away.*

*It felt like there was another reason for these interruptions, like her wanting to bring me back to the home environment. At one point I wondered whether she wanted my business to fail.*

*Some time after all this I spoke to a psychologist who thought my wife wouldn't be able to cope with the people I would meet if I was successful, therefore she wanted to make me less successful. At the time I was starting to network with lots of heads of industry and professionals and was on the brink of moving into very influential circles. I went to a reception once where the Prime Minister and American Ambassador were present. My wife wouldn't come with me. I had to take an escort instead. All this obviously brought up a lot of issues for her. The psychologist said she was also jealous of my success.*

*All this became a main feature of our subsequent divorce. She forced me to make a choice: my career or my family. She said the most important thing was the family, but I also wanted a career and the money while I was young. In the end I chose my career.*

*Working from home and running my own business high-lighted the problems in our marriage and brought them into focus. My wife was very competitive and jealous – even jealous of my relationship with our children.*

*We split up two and a half years after I went self-employed.*

A sad story, and one which highlights the very real potential pitfalls and the impact which working from home can have on relationships and family life, although Simon does point out that it wasn't just because of working from home that his marriage broke down. There were other factors. However, his homeworking obviously put an additional strain on the relationship and brought along with it other difficulties which eventually proved too much in their particular case.

When you live with other people, working from home is not just your issue, it affects everyone. The challenge is to try and make the effects as positive as possible, minimizing the potential for negative consequences and developing strategies for when they do.

## ■ WHAT WORKS

A US report which looked into the impact which home-based work had on the family (Carsky *et al.*, 1991) identified a number of issues which, they propose, lead to a more successful outcome in terms of quality of life and satisfaction levels for everyone. You're onto a winner when:

- the demands of the family interweave with the new work situation so that their needs are still met
- family members are able to make the necessary adjustments
- others feel that the support they can offer to the homeworker is important.

Looking back to Simon's experience it seems as though none of these occurred. His wife's needs were not met by Simon's working practice; the adjustments which perhaps both of them needed to make didn't come about successfully; and Simon clearly felt he received no support. Unfortunately we have only one side of the story, but it still highlights the fact that he felt unsupported and therefore could not provide his wife with the positive feedback she may have craved. The necessary give and take just didn't happen.

## ▪ MAKING IT WORK

In a way you're in a difficult position when you come to address the family. Starting out on homeworking, you're already mentally and emotionally half way down the road to your new venture and are probably fired with enthusiasm. But you have to turn back at some point and travel all the way back to the starting point in order to assemble your family or home group with the aim of rallying their support and have them come along as willing companions on the way. This can feel hard to do, but it is important. You can't force them or expect them to be able to make the giant leap on their own to where you are. Instead they will probably be feeling a bit confused at suddenly finding themselves assembled at the starting point of someone else's journey – yours. They'll be feeling a bit disorientated and lost. It's your task to recognize this and provide for them the sign-posts to enable them to find their way to join you, encouraging them and stopping every now and again to answer their questions and allay any fears they might have. They will probably spot obstacles, besides the ones you may have identified, and together you need to work out how they can be overcome.

These guidelines might help:

- Call a family meeting. Prepare yourself well beforehand. You need to have what you want to say and how you are going to say it set out very clearly before you.
- Explain to them what your plans are. This is where having worked out your aims and goals will come in useful. They will help to reassure them that there is a stable framework to what you are proposing.
- If homeworking is to be a stepping stone until you can afford other premises, let them know how long you intend this phase to last.
- Spell out the benefits to them of you being self-employed and of you working at home (be careful not to promise or say anything which you'll be unlikely to uphold once you get under way).
- Say what changes you think this might mean from your perspective.
- Say what you need and would like to be able to expect from them.

Now hand the floor over to them:

- Listen carefully (and as non-defensively as you can) to their reactions. If some of them are negative this may be difficult for you and your soaring enthusiasm. No one likes to have cold water thrown over their plans, but try to keep in mind the image of a somewhat confused group of individuals finding themselves at the start of someone else's journey (think about how you might feel if you found yourself in the same situation). At this moment it's your job to stay calm, generate a feeling of security and lead them safely through. They're not attacking you personally; they're just voicing their own concerns.

- Acknowledge their fears and worries. Try not to dismiss them out of hand – they're very real to them.
- It might help to note their concerns and worries on a note pad so that they will feel you are taking them seriously; it also might help make them feel they are part of the process.

Now for the hard part:

- Together, try to work out solutions to any problems or obstacles. Consider not only what you can do to enable them to make the adjustment to the new situation (or to kit them out for the journey, to stay with the analogy), but also consider what adjustments you will have to make, too (you may have to deal with the children at times, or go at a slower pace, etc.). Without compromising your self or your overall business aims, let them feel that you are keen to have them travel with you and that you will do what you can to make the journey enjoyable for everyone.
- Agree a modus operandi.
- Agree on dates and times for review meetings and put them in your diaries, with another agreement that these are fixed appointments that cannot be changed unless there is an emergency. This will help to encourage their commitment (and yours).

- You may need to have weekly meetings for the first couple of weeks, but later, as you all see fit, they can become fortnightly or monthly.
- Review meetings provide the opportunity to address and work through possible difficulties that may have emerged, and to decide on any changes that need to be made. They also enable you to give feedback on your progress, which will help them understand and feel part of the whole process even if they can't get much involved with the actual work itself.
- After agreeing the modus operandi you might want to spend some time thinking about what you can now do to reinforce important operational points. If you had not taken the time and made the effort to have a group discussion first, this would have been akin to turning up suddenly and telling family members to get their boots on because they were going for a walk (down the path of your journey). This would have led to misunderstanding and resentment. For example, expecting teenagers suddenly to start remembering to close doors quietly 'because you're working' would be unrealistic if you haven't first taken the time and care to explain why, giving them the chance to understand the new regime fully.

## Other Suggestions

- Let the family know your schedule.
- If you have to work quietly, pin notes to your door saying at what time you will be available if anyone needs to speak to you. A note saying simply 'Do Not Disturb' doesn't provide enough information or encourage much co-operation.
- Although you need to make others feel involved, try not to talk only about work all the time – I reckon this is one of the potential pitfalls for all homeworkers: becoming the home-base bore (more about how to avoid this in the next chapter).

- Consider how you can best make use of the flexibility which working at home brings, such as clocking off for an hour when the children come home, catching up on the time later by perhaps sending cheaper-rate faxes.
- It's been mentioned in other chapters, but do practise saying 'No' and refusing requests. It's important to be able to do so without then feeling guilty about it for the rest of the day.
- Learn how to be flexible without either compromising your sense of self or becoming a doormat.
- If they can't wait until your review meetings, leave talking through difficulties which have arisen until you're all more relaxed, and preferably away from home territory.

Accept that you will all go through a learning curve on this one. Give it time. It might also help to remind yourself that there is no such thing as a perfect person, including partners, family, friends and even (dare I say it?) you.

## ▪ CHILDREN

Working at home allows you the opportunity to combine a career with raising a family. Or so the thinking goes. To be honest, I'm not totally convinced about this one. If one equates running a business from home with other forms of employment, then where does raising children fit into the scheme of things when people are employees?

Either the primary-care parent works only part-time, or other provision is made for taking care of the children, whether that is organized by the parent in the form of nannies, nurseries or child-minders, or by the employer in the form of a crèche. Attending to young children appears to me to be a full-time job; expecting to do another full-time one on top seems a bit much.

Perhaps it is these expectations which might have to be analysed. If you find yourself run ragged and totally exasperated by coping with a teething child or a demanding two-year-old plus incoming sales enquiries at the same time, then it may be that a reassessment of the situation might present more workable solutions to take away some of the stress and pressure you may be under. You can't be expected to do everything all the time.

A change in attitude might also help. Perhaps accepting the amount of time which you can realistically give to the business and working with that might help. Instead of beating yourself up with worry because you're trying to fit in a 35-hour week, accept that after looking at the free time available (as in free from seeing to the children) there are really only 20 hours which you can guarantee. Scaling down your activities so that they fit in more easily with the available hours is more sensible, and you can always increase them as the children's demands decrease.

You may also have to look at what contribution your partner makes and whether a change there might help. For example, you might only be able to fit in four clear hours during a typical day, giving you 20 hours a week, but the remaining 15 hours (to make it full-time) might be found in the evenings or at weekends when your partner can take over the child-rearing and household reins. Work it out in terms of shifts. If you're both working full-time then you should both complete an equal number of house-/family-based shifts, too.

Alternatively, it is worth looking at the finances of the situation. Before you assume you can't afford child-care, make sure. For example, if you need 15 hours of child-care at £5 an hour, this will cost £75 a week. If you earn £15 an hour, you could make £225 in the same amount of time. See what I mean? Plus there will be the cost to the business in terms of lost time and opportunities; and there's also the cost to your sense of well-being.

If a nanny really does seem to be out of the question, think about compromising with a less expensive mother's help who could work more closely under your supervision. You might also consider sharing a nanny with another family.

Here are some other suggestions you might find useful:

- When a toddler starts to throw a tantrum, automatically put the answering machine on and return the calls when he has quietened down or is napping. A special cassette with a message to cover these situations might help, such as 'I'm in a meeting at present. Please try later, or if you prefer leave a message and I'll phone as soon as I'm free.' (Use your own words.) It's not quite so off-putting as the standard message we all tend to use, and it lets callers know you will be available shortly. Otherwise it's too easy for them to assume you've clocked off for the day and that they won't be able to get hold of you.
- Involve children in office play-work. Children like to feel involved, too. A four-year-old can spend hours doodling with some paper and a pen, banging away on your typewriter, or 'organizing' your books for you.
- Organize your work so that 'quiet' work is reserved for when your partner or child-carer is around.
- Clarify with older children which is their time and which is your time.
- Hang the cost – have a dedicated business line put in. It makes home life a lot simpler.
- Consider the merits for you and your business of a mobile phone.
- You may need some work 'rules', such as:
- No answering or using the business phone – even to contact you, unless in an emergency. You could miss that vital sales enquiry.

- No using your materials or equipment.
- And do explain, using age-appropriate words, why the rules have to be set. Provide alternatives to the No-go areas whenever possible.
- Devise training programmes for the kids so that they gradually become more self-sufficient about the house. It can start with the youngsters learning how to make their own sandwiches, through to older ones learning how to operate the washing machine. But perhaps you do this already . . .

## ▪ CHORES

What can I say? They have to be done. But the question which often arises for homeworkers is who shall do them, and when.

The enormity of the cultural change at home as you take up your new enterprise might take everyone by surprise. If it hasn't all been worked through in your initial family meetings, it will have to be worked through now. Of course if you were working full-time before you started working from home you may already have some kind of system in place. But if your responsibilities used to centre around the home you can't assume that your partner or other family members will automatically understand that you will now no longer be able to fit in three washes and two ironing sessions throughout the week. Even within families we all revolve within our own personal spheres of expectations, and when they aren't met it can create minor and even major havoc. Lest the situation degenerates into continual haranguing matches, you're going to have to take the initiative, call a house meeting and talk through any further changes which need to be made to accommodate everyone's needs – including your own. You might also have to spend some time, either on your own or with family members, devising ways to cut down on chores and/or find alternatives, not only when it comes to cleaning but also meals, maintenance, transport and so on. Start collecting household and gardening tips which you often see in some magazines and papers, or sift through books such as the *Reader's Digest Household Hints and Handy Tips*.

One alternative might be to employ housekeeping help. Again, balance the cost of a few hours a week against what it costs for you to take time out to do these chores. Include in the sums the cost to you and everyone else in terms of well-being, stress and family harmony.

## ■ FLATMATES

Unless you've already launched your business, consider carefully whether working from home is going to be viable in terms of the practicalities of balancing your needs against the needs of the others with whom you share. The only way to assess the situation is to talk it through with them and discuss any potential areas of difficulty, such as use of the phone, meeting clients, and holiday periods when other sharers are at home during the day. Think about it carefully and also give them time to think it over in more detail. With a wave of the hand they might casually say that it'll be fine, only to find later that they can't bear your fax machine waking them up in the early hours when they have to get up for an important breakfast meeting next day.

If the phone appears to be the only area of difficulty and you're sure you'll be staying put for a while, then consider having your own personal line installed, or use a mobile phone which offers a message-taking service for when you're not available.

If the situation looks too problematical it's best to put off homeworking until you're settled elsewhere, since relocating, even at this level, is still costly. If you found once you got started that you had to leave and set up in new premises, you would incur the expense of new stationery and notifying business contacts of the change. Valuable customers could easily be lost in the process.

## ▪ PARENTS

If you're still living with your parents the same basic strategies apply as for families in general – except that your parents hold the balance of power and can veto your plans at any time, so it is perhaps even more important for you to gain their support and commitment for your venture. To do that they need to understand fully what your homeworking idea is about:

- Follow the same guidelines as are laid out earlier in this chapter. Call a meeting and explain fully about: your aims; the benefits to them (really spell these out – they might need lots of reassurance); what impact it will have on the home; what you would like from them, not only in practical terms but also in the form of emotional and moral support.
- Think carefully about what you are going to say before you say it.
- Be prepared to modify your plans.
- If working at home is a stepping stone until you can afford your own premises, then work out how long this is realistically going to take. Knowing it will only be for a few months or a year might make it more palatable for them.
- Try not to be tempted into painting only half the picture. If stock is likely to be piled high in the hallway, then talk about this beforehand. You'll only create resentment and problems for yourself if you're not up-front about everything.

- If they're still unsure, then agree a trial period of, say, six months. Agree to have regular reviews with them, and let them know how things are faring.
- Once they agree, thank them. Take them out for treats every now and again – as any business person will tell you, you have to look after the people who are important to your business.

Handling the business side of working from home is only one (albeit vital) aspect of homeworking. What can really scupper the best-laid plans is what happens on the home front. Hopefully it won't lead to a situation like Simon's. You may have to tackle some tough sales situations in your new enterprise, but perhaps none will be so difficult as selling your ideas to your family and friends and gaining their support. If you can do that, then I'm sure you'll be on your way to a very successful future.

# 10 ▪ *Your Life Outside Work*

In the early days of working from home, your energies are so clearly focused on getting the business under way that little else seems to exist. Perhaps it has to be so during that first crucial period until things get on a more stable footing. It may be exciting, but it's also very demanding. A hundred and one things have to be done, and that doesn't even include finding customers or clients.

So perhaps it is understandable if one's social life grinds to a halt, and at best takes second place. Certainly it will undergo changes. The social interaction and subsequent invitations which form a natural part of many people's lives when they are employed suddenly disappear. So too does the sense of belonging. You may have detested the job, but you will have experienced a feeling of being part of some sort of group. That no longer exists. You're out there (or rather, in here) on your own. The casual socializing (the drink after work; the pub lunch) now just doesn't happen. But in the flurry of initial activity you may have hardly noticed the changes and the missing social element. Well, you haven't the time to miss it, have you? As Charles says, 'Because your office is "next door", you keep on working because 1) there's always something to do and 2) it is your own business and this personal stake drives you on.'

## ▪ THE DANGERS

Although this sort of narrow focus might be necessary in the early days, it can be a danger if it continues. And that can happen all too easily. Before you realize it you've developed certain work patterns and habits which have you steaming along at full tilt, seeing nothing much outside your business realm other than a visit to the accountant once in a while.

Then one day, when there's a lull in the work frenzy and you fancy going for a beer, it dawns on you that there's no one to go with. The friends and previous work colleagues who have attempted to keep in contact and draw you out every now and then have become tired of the excuses and the put-offs. They disappeared long ago to find better playmates. The gradual sense of isolation and loneliness, the only willing companion left, starts to nudge up against you. Your immediate circle of friends and contacts may have dramatically narrowed down.

William finds the interwoven nature of work and home can sometimes lead to withdrawing purposefully from social activities:

*The blurring of the line between home and work sometimes spills into my social life and I will put off going out because I know I can have an evening in on my own instead and then do a bit of work when I feel like it.*

He is wise, however, to the potential hazards of having this happen too frequently, and has developed a very active social life.

With the temptation of your job so close at hand it is easy to do a little more work rather than make an effort with your social life. The danger is that you run the risk of overworking and ending up demotivating yourself into the bargain. With being so blinkered and not casting your sights further afield than your desk diary, you also run the risk of becoming, how shall we say, a rather less than interesting person. Your work may have lots of facets which you love exploring, but to others you may come across as one-dimensional when conversation revolves around your work interests and little else. Ultimately this can lead to relationship problems. Other people's interest and tolerance levels might not extend to another rendition of 'How I made the most fantastic sale in the world.'

Another dangerous situation is when your reliance for social interaction falls on the shoulders of perhaps just one other, possibly your partner. We're complex people with a whole range of different needs; expecting one person to satisfy them all is asking for problems – not least of which is the risk of increasing frustration and resentment on the part of either party. If you feel that this other person really does fulfil all your needs, then perhaps this is because there are, as yet, vast areas of yourself lying hidden and unknown even to you. (And what fun you could have discovering them!)

The temptation to take the easy path, the one which leads to social laziness, is enormous. It's that much easier after the end of a long day simply to switch on the television and pour your-self a drink. No matter how little you say you need to socialize, the fact is that we all do need to every now and again. Not convinced? Read on.

## ▪ A CHANGE IS . . .

...As good as the proverbial rest – and just as necessary. Rest is something we all need when we're working hard on our home-based ventures. And hard it can be. So we need to find ways in which to recharge our batteries lest they become worn out and flat. Having a fulfilling social life can help with that recharging process.

Having some pleasant social activity looming on the horizon is highly motivating. It can help lighten the feelings of pressure on one of those Difficult Days by giving you something more pleasant to look forward to; a trip to the theatre to see a favourite play, perhaps, or even just a coffee with a friend. It becomes a sort of self-induced reward system.

Non-work activities scattered throughout the weeks remind you that there are pleasant things in life. It isn't all hard graft and nose to the bank book – or it doesn't have to be.

But being the business-minded person you undoubtedly are (otherwise you wouldn't be self-employed) you might be wondering whether socializing can benefit not just yourself but also your business.

By being pro-active in making arrangements to see friends you can avoid the difficulties of them popping round unexpectedly or pestering you at the wrong moment. You might find it a useful way in which to cut out such unwelcome interruptions. And if they do call, it makes it that much easier to suggest that what they have to say might wait until your next evening out.

Another spin-off to socializing is that you may also make some useful business contacts, either directly or indirectly: the chap you met at bridge classes has a brother who sounds like the supplier you've been hunting for; the chair of the club you've joined has a husband who's been looking for an expert widget-maker.

But for me, the most important benefit of socializing is to my sense of well-being; and without that, how well can you expect to work at your business?

## ▪ GETTING IT UNDER WAY

Spend a moment or two reviewing the present range of activities in your life which take you outside the home or otherwise bring you into immediate contact with other people. Some of these may be work related. Make a note of how often the different activities take place (refer to your diary or ask others for their help in recalling past meetings).

Now analyse what you have. It will probably be obvious where any gaps are when you realize the last social visit outside the home was to see how Auntie Flo was getting on – two months ago. Don't beat yourself up about it if that's the case. No doubt you've had lots to do and work and family have been your priorities. (But might you be feeling a little bit frayed around the edges because of it?) Use the opportunity to consider the present balance you have between work and your social life, how happy you feel about it and what improvements you would ideally like to see. .

## Problem Areas

If you find yourself up against some real obstacles to making better use of your spare time, you might need to draw on your problem-solving skills (Chapter 8). You might also benefit from employing your time-management skills, too. What you have learned about managing your work time effectively can also be applied to your social time. Take William's example: 'Every month I make sure I've seen and done certain things – six films/two plays/one exhibition, for example.' Charles offers this advice: 'Set a "stop time" every day (clients permitting). Get out at least once a week for leisure of any kind – that is, *remove yourself* from the premises.' And Carol also realizes she has to be pro-active: 'I try to plan ahead, scheduling theatre/dinner parties/evenings out, and keep a check on myself and alert myself to when I am being too reclusive.'

If family commitments seem to make it more difficult for you to get things organized, you may have to discuss the issue with your partner or even the whole family. You might consider taking a half day off for social activities during the day when children are at school or with child-minders, and then making up the time in the evening after they've settled down; or even spreading the four extra hours over the rest of the week, adding an hour to each working day.

You might also want to have a look again at the household chores. It's too easy for them to sneak in and lay claim to the only bit of free time you seem to have away from your work. If necessary, be brutal. See if chores can be redistributed more fairly or whether other ways around them can be found (see Chapter 7). Use your problem-solving skills to help you.

## Some Suggestions

You may be content with deciding to make more regular contact with your existing network of friends. On the other hand, even with a bulging address book you may decide that you would like some input from other sources and to take part in activities which take you completely away from work (talk with friends can often still revolve around work issues). Some people like to choose something practical if their heads are buried in books and intellectual pursuits all day, while a more manual worker might choose to join a class to learn a language. It's all part of the internal balancing act. Spend some time reflecting on what you feel would provide a good counterpoint to your own normal work and family-based activities.

The thought of groups of any kind can seem intimidating, yet most make newcomers only too welcome. With other groups, which might be used to seeing people simply passing through, you might have to show your intended commitment by turning up a few times on the trot. In any case, I suggest that with any new group you join you make sure you do attend fairly regularly for the first few occasions to give others the chance to recognize you and for you to become more of a familiar face. Otherwise you will feel reluctant to go if you know you'll have to start the whole introduction process again, and it will take you that much longer to form any sort of meaningful links. However, even with the best will sometimes a group's dynamics, membership or activities can turn out to be a damp squib so far as you're concerned. It happens. If you do think it's a dead duck then bow out gracefully and investigate some of the other activities you're interested in. Consider these:

- Investigate the opportunities available through your children's schools. There may be committees you could join; you could also make yourself available for helping to run or organize special events.
- Look into the volunteer opportunities in your locality. It has been shown that helping others can, paradoxically, help your-self. There's a vast range available, from digging someone's garden for them to being a reader for talking newspapers. Pay a visit to your local volunteer bureau or get more information from your local library, town hall or Citizens Advice Bureau.
- Local committees and charities abound to provide you with opportunities for socializing through the contacts you make and the events they organize. Becoming involved in the volun-tary sector also provides you with a means by which you can put something back into the society in which you work and live. You may find it provides you with new challenges and a different perspective on life.
- Investigate the arts-based opportunities in your area. Apart from trips to the theatre, you may find they also run courses. Besides watching the local drama productions, what about joining in (perhaps backstage if the footlights don't appeal)? Art classes are an obvious one, but what about the offerings of your local/nearest art gallery? There may also be poetry groups, film clubs, writer's circles . . . Your local library should

be able to advise you on what is on offer.

- Becoming more actively involved in religious or spiritual activities can provide you with opportunities for socializing and making new friends, and can also help improve your sense of well-being. There may also be other social activities related to the group providing yet more chances of becoming involved.

- Working on the land or aiming to help the environment might be more your scene. The British Trust for Conservation Volunteers provides opportunities to work on environmental projects, literally at grassroots level! Bird-watching groups might offer possibilities, or perhaps you can help out at local animal care centres and shelters.

- Owning a pet can offer ways in which to socialize, too, in part but not only through joining clubs and attending shows, as Gilly found out when she acquired her labrador: 'Regular outings with my "furry companion" has meant more exposure of a sort, and friendships with local folk have developed as a result.'

- Sport is an obvious suggestion, but you might also like to consider some of the less obvious activities which may be available in your area, including skill-based sports such as archery or clay-pigeon shooting. There may also be a related club or society to join which can offer additional social occasions.

- Pressure groups and local politics are other areas which might appeal to some. They frequently organize social functions, and you will be helping to influence or join the fight for what you believe is right.

- On the holiday front, activity holidays provide better opportunities for meeting people than does lying on the beach with your eyes closed for two weeks!

- If really you're looking for a partner, do consider dating agencies and marriage bureaux. Many professional people who, like you, don't have the normal range of social opportunities at their disposal use them.

As for activities which are rather more work-related:

- Joining in with professional groups and activities can lead to other social opportunities, and since you will have a shared interest with the other people present you might find new friendships developing. Find out what is available near you.
- Devise and organize social events for your business, such as a wine and cheese evening for your customers, held at a local venue.
- Develop a sideline business activity which enables you to socialize more. For example, Barry is hoping to do some lecturing as an off-shoot of his writing career.
- Find out about any training courses you might attend. Not only will it benefit you professionally by extending your range of skills and knowledge, but I find that training groups can gel and develop socially more quickly than others.

You may find that because you are working on your own at home you miss that important sense of belonging which we all need to feel. Although friends and family might fill the void to a certain extent, in all but the remotest areas other opportunities do exist for building these very important social networks. In the main, opportunities won't fall into your lap and a certain amount of effort and work are necessary (in terms of making initial enquiries or fixing dates with existing friends). But I believe the benefits to you, your sense of well-being and ultimately your business make all the work well worth it. All work and no play…

## 11 ▪ *Fit for Work*

**W**e leave nothing to chance. Our business depends on how we keep the books, look after customers, maintain the equipment we use. We check the health of the bank account, keep it in balance, attend regularly to our budgets. So anxious are we that our business succeeds that we keep a tender, watchful eye on all its different aspects at all times, planning, monitoring and, if necessary, taking preventative action. But what of the other vital ingredient: ourselves? It's far too easy to plough on regardless, demanding of ourselves 100 per cent (sometimes more) with scant regard to the impact our behaviour and actions are having on our physical and mental health. To put it mildly, we take ourselves for granted.

Yet without someone to operate all those wonderful business checks and monitoring procedures, and without someone to provide the service, make the product and find the customers, there is no business. It halts, stops, finishes. It is no more.

In the past, when we became ill as an employee we may have been concerned about what would happen in our absence, but ultimately we knew that the Great Machine would keep on turning. Urgent work would be covered by others and somehow everyone would muddle through until we returned; no one the worse – not even financially.

Running your own enterprise is very different. If there's no you to do the urgent work it probably just doesn't get done. Neither do you get paid. You're talking to someone who had to spend two months literally on the floor because of a gradual-onset slipped disc – all brought about through poor work practices. I've learned the hard way, but hopefully this chapter will help you avoid having to do the same.

## ■ WHERE YOU'RE AT

It might be of assistance to you to gain a fuller insight into where you're at right now in terms of how you look after yourself. Spend a few moments to reflect on how you operate throughout the day; the range of activities you take part in; how you feel at the end of each day and week; the positive things you do to look after yourself; the money you set aside to spend on looking after yourself. (Compare this with the money you have spent on your car over the last year.) Use your time-management diary to prompt your memory if it all seems a blur. If that doesn't give you enough information you might like to consider monitoring yourself for a day or so. If you can't manage even this, consider what this tells you about the importance you place on yourself. Remember: without you there is no business.

Until you know where you're really at you won't have a very clear picture of where any improvements need to be made.

## ■ PREVENTION

Prevention has to be the aim when you're in business on your own. The prospect of being ill while working at home may not seem too daunting (you can imagine you'll probably be able to teeter into your home office for a while), but that isn't really the point. Being ill will still have an impact on your business. Trying to ignore ill-health and working through it will mean you will be running at only half-steam or less, making matters worse; and there is always the danger when you carry on working of never quite managing to shrug off whatever illness you've contracted. Weeks and even months later you're still feeling under the weather, struggling to find your way back to good health. This will all affect your blossoming enterprise. It will also affect your bank balance.

Taking sensible health precautions should help reduce the risk of being laid up. Make a belated New Year's Resolution straight away to make prevention your health watchword from now on.

## ▪ WHERE YOU WORK

One of the attractions of running a business from home is that you can start tomorrow (or today, even) with nothing more elaborate than a good idea and a kitchen table to work at.

Yes, it has to be admitted that it seems to make sense to use as many of the available resources you have, at least to get you going. Unfortunately, inadequate facilities can eventually do the opposite and end up bringing you to a grinding halt. That is what happened to me.

### Desks, Chairs and Work Surfaces

Like many people, in order to keep initial outlay costs down I made do with what was to hand. As a writer I didn't need any special facilities, just somewhere where I could sit and work at the computer. I decided to use a writing bureau I have. It seemed the most logical (though in retrospect not the most sensible) place since it contained my stationery, files and other bits and pieces which I used during my work. It also provided a work surface. Granted it was a bit too shallow to put the computer on, but I soon solved that problem by placing it on the top part of the bureau instead; except that because of all the connectors which stuck out the back against the wall I had to move it to one side and put it at an angle, otherwise there wasn't quite enough space for it. There. Now for the seating.

There wasn't much to choose from, really: a couple of Lloyd loom chairs which were very comfortable but a bit too low; a folding chair which wasn't comfortable at all; and a bentwood dining chair. The dining chair won. It was a bit high and although it was pretty it didn't offer anything much in the way of back support – but it would do. I was set. My writing career was launched.

All was fine for quite a while. There was the odd bit of stiffness after I'd done 'a stint', but I suppose that was only to be expected after, gosh, has it really been two hours? And then it got worse. And worse. And then I couldn't move at all.

It wasn't until I acquired a proper office chair and desk that I realized what I must have been doing to my poor body. Everything had become strained from holding my head at an awkward angle to see the screen which was too high and off to one side; sitting without back support and leaning forward because there wasn't much space for my knees to go very far underneath the work surface wreaked havoc with my back; holding my arms at the wrong angle because the bureau was too high did my shoulders in; and tensing my legs because the chair was too high put paid to my legs as well. I was a physical wreck! Now it feels positively heavenly to sit in comfort, and I can hardly believe the effect on my recovering slipped disc.

So, all the warnings about having good seating and work surfaces are true. Let's run through them again:

### The Chair
An office chair is best if you have to sit down for any length of time. It should conform to the following standards:

- Its height should be adjustable.
- The height should be set so that your feet are flat on the floor or footrest.
- It should have a back rest which can be adjusted forwards, backwards, and up and down.
- The back rest should give good support to your lower back.
- It should have a stable base.
- A seat tilting mechanism is ideal, too.
- Whether it has arms or not depends on the type of work you do. It is generally accepted that without arms is best if you work solely at a keyboard, for example with data entry work.

**The Work Surface**
- It should be of a height so that your forearms are horizontal to the floor when you are using the keyboard.
- It should allow sufficient room for your legs to fit comfortably underneath.

**The Computer**
- The top of the screen should be at about eye-height.
- It should have brightness and contrast controls.
- The keyboard should be positioned so that your wrists are supported when you are not keying.
- The screen should ideally have a tilt and swivel facility.

Finding the right chair and work surface shouldn't be too difficult or costly. I made a few discreet enquiries and found a business which had recently scaled down its operations and had a store of excess furniture. Since the chair I wanted had a broken castor and a wobbly arm (soon remedied afterwards with a screwdriver) they let me have it for free. Then some simple measurements to work out what my working height was, a trip to the local hardware store for some chipboard cut to size, and a simply assembled desk was born. The whole arrangement must have cost me no more than the equivalent of one hour's work, yet it has proved to be my most valuable investment yet.

If you want professional help in setting up a new workstation consult a qualified ergonomist or occupational physiotherapist (Ergonomics Society, 01509 234904; Association of Chartered Physiotherapists in Occupational Health, 0171–242 1941). They will help measure you up and advise on the best working set-up for you, on any changes you need to make to an existing one, and what you should be looking for in any furniture you buy.

Although most references to work areas relate to 'desk jobs', the same applies to any work surface used in other types of businesses. For example, if you're a baker you need to have your work surface at an appropriate height so that you don't have to bend too low or strain your arms and shoulders because it is too high. Work out what is best for the type of activities your business involves you in.

Appropriate work areas are incredibly important. Because of the inefficiency of mine I damaged my back; other people have developed the equally disabling Repetitive Strain Injury. At the very least you may start to suffer from headaches, tension, sore shoulders or a more general feeling of discomfort. These are the first signs that all is not well, and all I would suggest is that you do something about it straight away to avoid the possibility of greater troubles building up later on.

## ▪ LIGHTING

As employees we tend to take for granted such things as lighting in our place of work. In working at home the tendency is to accept the available lighting provision as it is and forget to reassess it in terms of how adequate it is for its new purposes. Inadequate or inappropriate lighting can cause unnecessary eye-strain, leading in the longer term to possible eye problems, headaches and tension. It's worth giving a moment's thought to the adequacy of your lighting system.

- Place computer screens so that they do not have any direct light shining on them, including sunlight. The reflections and glare cause eye-strain, slow down your work and increase the chances of mistakes. Ambient light is better. Try flooding lights upwards to reflect off the ceiling.
- Spotlights need careful adjustment so that they are not directly shining on the screen or into your eyes, or creating shadows as you lean over your work.
- An adjustable desk lamp provides directed light just where you need it.
- Ordinary light bulbs have a yellow cast. Daylight simulation bulbs, which give a blue, and more natural light, are now widely available from good electrical stores. They are particularly helpful to artists and graphic designers as they allow colours to be seen more accurately.
- Without even the daily trek to the office, homeworking can mean we run the risk of not getting enough exposure to daylight. For some people this can develop into Seasonal Affective Disorder where their moods become badly affected. Full spectrum lighting can help. Besides the light-boxes which are used to treat the disorder, there are also overhead strips available.

## ▪ VENTILATION

At first it can be difficult to appreciate that just because you are now working at home your ordinary domestic arrangements are not necessarily going to suffice. You need to move away from simply accepting that 'The dining chair will do. I've sat in it to eat meals for the last five years and had no problems,' or 'There's nothing the matter with this overhead light.' The same goes for ventilation.

Normally the windows may stay firmly closed until the heat of summer strikes or when the fishy cooking smells run riot, but when you're working all day at home, perhaps always in the same room, you need to have some fresh air circulating around. This doesn't mean flinging the windows wide so a gale blows through, leaving you shivering. Have one open a few centimetres or so, just to help keep the room clear of staleness and any fumes which might be coming off equipment you might be using. You'll feel better for not working in a stuffy, oxygen-starved environment and it should help you stay more alert throughout the day. Obviously ventilation is even more important if you use noxious chemicals in your work, including some proprietary office cleaning and art materials.

Ionizers also help keep the air charged with beneficial negative ions – especially important when you're frequently using electrical equipment. You may want to consider using one where you work to help keep you feeling more refreshed.

## ▪ HOW YOU WORK

It's not only where you work that's important, but also how you work – that is, your work patterns, practices and habits. The danger is that if these are not particularly good or healthy you run the risk of them affecting your overall sense of well-being and your efficiency. In turn, this will affect your business – and your bank balance.

## Fresh Air

We've just mentioned the importance of having adequate ventilation in your place of work, but it is also important to try and get out into the fresh air at least once a day. A few deep breaths can do wonders for clearing the brain and refreshing those parts which probably need refreshing. It will help recharge your batteries and increase your work efficiency. If possible, combine it with a stroll to get the circulation going, especially if you have been sitting for a long period of time. Even when the sun isn't shining we benefit from direct exposure to daylight.

You might also like to use your fresh air fix to serve as a buffer between the start and/or end of your working day. It needn't be a long hike – just an amble to the shop for a paper will do.

## Breaks

Regular breaks are vital when you're working. They are so important that there are laws to make employers comply. When you're self-employed you are your own employer, and as such you need to make sure you give yourself adequate breaks and rest periods. This is particularly important if you do a lot of keyboard or other work which involves you in continuous, repetitive movements. Without regular breaks the muscles and tendons which are constantly being used can become strained, leading to Repetitive Strain Injury.

Having breaks can be difficult to get into at first because the temptation is to do just that little bit more; finish this off; just make a start on that; and then another hour's flown by. In the normal work environment we experience so many interruptions from colleagues and making trips to the next office that we tend to get a better quota of breaks. At home, the situation can be very different.

Until you've got into the habit, you may need to 'train' yourself to take these short breaks. Use a kitchen timer and set it to go off after 20 minutes. This is how often you should move around if you sit in the same position for any length of time, to help avoid stiffness creeping in and your circulation coming to a near halt. This doesn't mean you should then spend half an hour taking a rest break and making another cup of coffee; it just means you should get up and walk across the room, stretch your body a bit, and move it around (in the seat if necessary). Then about every 90 minutes, have a proper break for 10 minutes or so to give yourself a fuller recharging. Once you get into the habit you will probably find it helps you get through the day more easily, and that your work efficiency increases.

Think of yourself as a finely tuned engine which, at the start of the day, hums along nicely. Without a break to recharge, the hum slowly degenerates into a whine. Give yourself the breaks your body needs and you should still be humming along nicely come close of day.

## Balance

Because work is the focus, it is so easy to let things slip out of balance – but once they do it can have dire effects on both you and your business. Managing to attain and maintain that all-important perspective can be a real challenge when it seems more important than anything else to keep your nose to that grindstone.

Analysing how you work will help, and as part of that process you should spend some time considering elements of your present life and whether you feel they are in any sort of working balance. You might like to use doodles to help you see more clearly what, for example, the ratio is between work and play:

Make other doodles which represent other elements, such as:

| | |
|---|---|
| Creative activities: | Uncreative activities |
| Family pressures: | Family support |
| Inactivity: | Exercise |
| Social activities: | Solitary activities |
| Family time: | Me time |

Spend a few moments reflecting on other areas, relevant to your own personal circumstances, which could be illustrated in this way, then have a look at what your doodles tell you. They should clearly indicate where there are imbalances in your life and help you see which need some attention. Remember too that what goes on in your non-work hours will affect your work, and vice versa, so make sure you've not just looked at work-related activities.

## ▪ PRESSURE

We all experience it from time to time: rush jobs to do; deadlines to meet; a last-minute sales call to handle. It's part and parcel of being self-employed. However, if this becomes an habitual way of working then you're heading for trouble and a case of burnout. We've already looked at overworking in Chapter 5, but you may need to consider again whether your working and personal life are pressurizing you too much. If you feel this is the case then use the problem-solving techniques in Chapter 8 to help you find ways around some of the problem areas. Also, make sure you're using your time-management techniques to the full. More serious attempts at expert planning and scheduling might alleviate many of the pressures you might be experiencing.

### Support

We've already mentioned support in chapters 6 and 7. It really is vital to make the fullest use of all available sources and types of help. You may find it useful to reflect again on whom and what you use, and stay alert to developing situations which might call for investigations into what other sources of help might be available and necessary.

Although the business is your responsibility, it doesn't mean you should carry all the burdens singlehanded. Modifying your work practices in this way may benefit both you and your business enormously, giving you more time to take those all-important breaks during the day and maintain a healthy balance in your life.

## *Inputs*

Running your own show means you are giving out all the time, and sometimes it can feel like you've been giving more than just the 100 per cent. Besides the other suggestions in the rest of the chapter, take a moment or two to think about what inputs you have in your life to help balance up the picture. Inputs can be anything which you feel gives you energy and replenishes your sense of well-being. Here are some of my inputs:

- books
- going to the theatre
- friends
- sketching
- walking in the park
- cooking
- my cat
- luxuriating in a long, hot bubble bath
- going for a massage
- trips to art galleries.

Draw up a list of your inputs. If you feel it's a case of 'Could do better,' then start to investigate ways in which you could start to introduce more inputs which nourish, enrich and revitalize you. Not only do you deserve them, they are also important if you are going to be able to handle the normal stresses and strains which being self-employed can put on you.

## ▪ EATING

Food. Without it we grind to a halt, so it's important to make sure you're fuelling yourself (and ultimately your business) in the best possible way. We need good food if we are to work well

– snacking on sweeties throughout the day does *not* constitute good food. Here are some suggestions:

- Avoid snacking on biscuits and odd bits picked at here and there from the fridge, cupboard and cake tins. If you're already leading a more sedentary life because of working at home, then extra weight will go on even more easily. Eat proper meals instead and fuel your body in a more healthy and nourishing way.
- Now that you have access to full cooking facilities throughout the day you may wish to consider totally revamping your eating habits. There is the old saying that one should breakfast like a king, lunch like a lord and dine like a pauper. I must admit it seems to make sense to provide your body with the energy it needs at the start of the day rather than leaving it until the evening when really it's not needed in the same way. If you haven't eaten all day then of course you will be hungry by then, but how much more sensible to make sure your body has the fuel it needs earlier on.
- If you don't want to spend time cooking at midday, satisfying lunches can easily be made by throwing a bowl of salad together and eating it with chunks of wholemeal bread. You might also like to make a large pan of homemade soup which can then be eaten over a number of days, again served with fresh crusty wholemeal bread. Delicious, and full of lots of goodness. Real five-star fuel.
- If you're at all in doubt about whether you get your quota of vitamins and minerals, I think it is worth spending money on some top-quality supplements, regardless of what they might say about getting what you need from a normal, balanced diet. If the foods we ate were fresh direct from their natural source, perhaps, but personally I'm not convinced otherwise.
- Do watch the amount of tea, coffee and cola you drink. The

tea is mildly diuretic which means you can become slightly dehydrated if you drink copious amounts, and the caffeine in coffee and cola drinks increases the adrenalin in your bloodstream. This is fine to give you a boost in the morning, but drinking too much coffee during the day can leave you feeling jittery and sleepless at night, and is also linked to panic attacks. Switch to decaffeinated teas and coffees, mineral water and fruit juices – and try some herbal teas, too.

## ▪ EXERCISE

This is one of the vital ingredients in making sure you stay fit for work. It benefits not only your body but also your mind by providing a way in which to switch off from thinking about work all the time.

As has already been mentioned, during the working day you need to make sure you move about and change position on a regular basis. Use lunch breaks or after-work time to include more involved activities. You could commandeer a neighbour's dog to walk on a regular basis, which would benefit you, the dog – and your neighbour. You might also learn some simple exercise routines to do at home. There are lots of videos and books now available. Or you might like to learn yoga or T'ai Chi movements. Think about the different types of exercise and how they might benefit you personally. You can use vigorous sports to enliven, or gentle exercise to help you relax. Both will help you discharge harmful tensions which might have accumulated during the day.

Because you may have become more sedentary since working at home, it really is important to introduce exercise into your new working life. It needn't necessarily involve the use of a gym;

simple walking will suffice. Use your time-management techniques to help you schedule it into your week's activities. It might even provide a useful way in which to stay in touch with friends as well.

## ■MENTAL HEALTH

Although being physically healthy is important, so too is being mentally healthy. Stress and worries can easily take hold and affect your sense of well-being, so it is crucial that you keep a watchful eye on your work practices to make sure you are treating yourself well. No one can work effectively if feeling depressed or over-anxious.

Pay attention to stresses coming from different sources. They can be internally generated, related to interpersonal difficulties, related to your locality or affected by the nature of the work you do, aside from the general day-to-day business worries.

If you make sure you are handling your working practices effectively, using the support which is available and maintaining a healthy balance in your life you should minimize the effects of these stresses. But if you feel the problems are a result of inter-personal or internal difficulties and that you could do with a helping hand to sort them out, have a word with your doctor to see about what counselling support services are available in your area. If the worries are purely work-related, go back to Chapter 6 to read about the professional support which might be available to help.

## ▪ PREVENTATIVE TREATMENT

Doctors can give you a health check, but they only tend to pick up problems once they've occurred. How much better to take evasive action and pinpoint any imbalances in your body's energy flow beforehand. There are a number of therapeutic treatments which will facilitate this, and it may well be worth your while investigating some of them to find ways in which you can lovingly take care of your body. You might like to consider some of these:

- Alexander Technique: to ensure you are using your body and its available energies wisely.
- Shiatsu: rebalances the body's energies and gently mobilizes any blockages before they start to cause ill-health.
- Reflexology: works on the body's energies through gently manipulating areas on the soles of the feet.
- Iridology: can pinpoint potential trouble spots through a detailed examination of the eyes. Various treatments and therapies are then recommended.
- Massage: can really get rid of all those stresses and strains which have accumulated in the body's muscle tissues. By helping to discharge them it helps to prevent other related problems from developing.

## ▪ HEALTH AND SAFETY

As a self-employed person you are legally responsible for your own health and safety at work, and also for ensuring that you don't put others at risk. If you've never had to consider these issues before, contact the Health and Safety Executive (HSE) which can advise you on any particular precautions you should be taking in your own work. They have free leaflets available, including one entitled *Working With VDUs* (HSE Information Centre, Broad Lane, Sheffield S3 7HQ; 0114 289 2346.)

Here are some basic health and safety checkpoints:

- Check that you are using appropriate protective clothing, including goggles, gloves, ear protectors, masks, boots and overalls as necessary.
- If you use chemicals and noxious substances, send for the health and safety data sheets from the manufacturers.
- Make sure there are no trailing cables across areas where people tread. It's better to use extension leads and run them along the edge of the room. If leaving them across the floor cannot be avoided, tape the cables to the floor with broad tape. Do not put them underneath carpets – you need to be able to access them quickly and to spot if the outer casing becomes damaged.
- Check you have the correct fuses in the plugs of any equipment you use. A 13-amp fuse is only appropriate for some pieces of equipment – not all.
- Make sure you have a first-aid kit to hand.

## ▪ INSURANCE

Hopefully illness or accident will not be something you encounter, but it is probably a wise precaution to consider the benefits of taking out insurance to cover you against the risk. The two types you may want to consider are:

- Health insurance: The Hospital Savings Association (*see*

Appendix B for address) operates a scheme whereby you receive a lump sum should you have to be hospitalized. The money can be used as you wish, either to pay for private treatment or to provide a basic income while you are out of commission. Through this scheme they also refund a percentage of the fees you may have had to pay to dentists, physiotherapists, opticians, and others.

- There are, of course, other schemes which simply pay for private hospital treatment. Many choose to opt for private health care to avoid the problem that can occur with the NHS in Britain of having to wait for long periods of time before receiving treatment. You might want to consider the impact that a long wait while unable to work would have on your business.
- Income protection: This provides you with an income should you fall ill or have an accident. This is particularly important when you are self-employed since no work means no pay – not even Sickness Benefit, in the UK.
- Your insurance broker should be able to advise you about available policies, but check out other sources, too. Lloyds Bank, for example, currently offer an income-protection policy in their range of insurance products.

Being self-employed makes you incredibly vulnerable should anything happen to you which makes you incapable of work for any length of time. Taking out private health insurance means that, should you need treatment you will be able to receive it quickly and therefore resume work as soon as possible, minimizing the effect on your business. Think about your insurance needs very carefully and take the steps which you feel are most appropriate for your individual situation. Unless you have massive savings on which to draw, then at least some form of basic cover is essential.

The move to working from home will mean many changes take place. It is too easy to overlook both the impact which these changes may have on you and also the compensations you need to make to your new way of working. You are the most important aspect of the business; its greatest asset. Make sure you look after this particular investment, and do learn from my experience – but please, please don't repeat it!

# 12 ■ *An Opportunity for Growth*

The sails are up on your new ship *Enterprise*, all set for the winds of fortune to take you into new, uncharted seas. The excitement runs high as you leave the predictable, secure world behind where limits were only too recognizable and real challenges rare. Now you're pushing back the boundaries and seeking fresh horizons in which to explore the newfound freedom to dance to your own tune rather than someone else's. You sigh in contentment as the new light dawns on you that yes, you can at last be yourself; the captain of your own soul and destiny.

There's just one little question, though. What exactly does 'being yourself' actually mean? Come to think of it, you might find yourself wondering who you really are. Within the predictable confines of your existence up to now you have probably come to know yourself pretty well. Routines were established and carried out; occasional highlights were thrown in every now and again just to keep your interest going. Now things are very different. You've cast aside the safety and security of what was for the excitement of what may be.

Whatever work we do provides us with opportunities to learn about ourselves. Unsatisfactory jobs are those which provide few opportunities to stretch and challenge ourselves; we become bored. By entering self-employment you also enter one of the best arenas in which to learn about yourself and your capabilities. You can start to uncover, disclose and investigate your actions to find out which ones help and hinder your self-esteem, rate of progress and sense of well-being. With self-employment you have found for yourself the perfect self-development scenario to help you become a better you.

## ▪ WHY HOMEWORKING IS SO CHALLENGING

Since essentially there is only you involved in your home business you will find that suddenly you have to wear many other hats besides just the one which says 'graphic designer' or 'financial adviser'. Now you may have to be stationery monitor, public relations executive, secretary, bookkeeper, telephonist, manager, sales executive and so on, all in the course of the working week. These have to be interchanged with domestic roles at the flick of a switch as you leave your work area and enter the family domain.

Also, since there is only you, you will probably find yourself in lots of situations which you would otherwise never have encountered, let alone had to manage. Previously it would have been handled by Anne in sales, Jerry in customer service or even The Boss for the really big problems and front-line situations. As you cast your eye around your work area, hoping to find someone else to send, it comes home to you yet again that since the cat is far too preoccupied with chasing butterflies then it has to be you. The buck stops right in front of none other than yours truly. And it stays there.

## ▪ ISSUES WHICH MAY BE ENCOUNTERED

As you find yourself launched into these many different roles and situations it will become clear that some present real difficulties while others make you feel utterly exhilarated. There isn't the space in this book to go into each situation you might meet, but it may be useful to have a general look at the types of personal issues that you might come across.

## Personal Strengths

Let's start with the positive. We all have personal strengths which we unconsciously draw on and use to help propel us forward in life. Unfortunately many can often go unnoticed. Spend some time reflecting on your own personal strengths. Include, but also think beyond, the obvious skill or expertise which is the foundation for your business. If you are also good with people, put that down too. If you have an excellent telephone manner, include that. If you receive compliments on the sales letters you send out, that counts as well. Make a point of noting down the things you see yourself doing well, and make it an ongoing feature of your daily work to do so. What you will find is that you have a whole range of abilities, many of which you may have taken for granted and possibly under-used.

This sort of self-awareness has a point: when you become more aware of what you're good at it is that much easier to devise work patterns that get the most out of you for your business, at the least personal cost to yourself. For example, if you love telephone work make your next sales push focus on telesales. If you hate the telephone but revel in devising appealing sales literature then do it that way. But until you know your strengths it will be difficult to gear your work accordingly.

## Weaknesses

Yes, we all have them. Most of the time we spend lots of precious energy trying to cover them up and pretend they're not there. As with your strengths, it is useful to know your own weaknesses well. Instead of hiding away from them, acknowledge them. It isn't until we do that we can start to take remedial action to compensate in a positive way for what we may lack in certain areas. Pretending we can do everything when it's quite patently obvious that we can't does no one any good – least of all ourselves because of the amount of pressure it puts us under. So be kind and accept that, for example, the telephone isn't really your best communication tool. Once you accept and acknowledge a personal limitation, feel the tension around it disappearing. With the energy you release you can now do something about it, perhaps by signing yourself onto a 'How to Use the Telephone Effectively' course.

Just as you are doing with your strengths, spend time also noting down your weaknesses. Acknowledging them doesn't mean you are less of a person or a useless geek, just that you're human – like the rest of us. Ultimately this enables you to transform the situation and do something positive to help work with your weaknesses instead of using so much of your energy trying to avoid them.

## Internal Blocks

Blocks prevent us from moving forward and becoming more truly who we are. There are many ways in which they may have developed within us, and as you encounter a wider range of people, experiences and challenges you may find yourself suddenly up against one of them. The block may be there as a result of family or social conditioning, such as 'No daughter of mine is going to earn her living doing that,' or 'People from your cultural background or class don't do that sort of work.' Sometimes the blocks are the result of your own past experiences leading you to believe that because you once found something difficult then you will continue to find it so for ever, without ever stopping to think that it may have been because the tutor was inefficient or you just weren't ready for the challenge at that moment in your life.

Too easily we take in these messages and experiences and cast them in stone. All they then serve to do is weigh us down and prevent us from seeing ourselves in a truer light.

Next time you find yourself up against any internal blocks which are stopping you from moving forward, try to find out what they are about. Once you know what they are, it becomes easier to do something about them.

## ∎ INTERPERSONAL RELATIONSHIPS

At some point during the course of running your home business you will come across difficult situations with others. You will probably be dealing with a wide range of people, all making various demands on you and all having different expectations of you, too. Conflict is bound to arise at some point.

It is through learning how to handle conflict that we discover a great deal about ourselves. It's a sobering thought that those characteristics we find most unpleasant and difficult to handle or accept in other people tend to be ones which are reflected in ourselves.

Dealing with conflict arouses emotions; how you deal with these can be either harmful or helpful. Suppressing them is generally harmful, yet it can be a real challenge to find helpful ways in which to release them. But released they must be, otherwise they may cause untold damage at a later date. Simply giving voice to your emotions helps tremendously; sometimes this is accompanied by automatic physical releases like crying. Cathartic methods help release pent-up feelings, too, which it may not have been possible to release at the time. Writing down how you feel, thrashing cushions or shouting and screaming at a mattress while you punch it all provide outlets for the pent up emotional energy. Finally, emotions can be transformed into something positive, such as creating a work of art or using the energy to launch a project which is linked to rectifying the situation that has caused the difficulty.

It is incredibly important to find your own way of being able to release your emotions. Unexpressed negative ones are thought to be the root cause of many, and some say all, illnesses. At the very least, holding them in means that you are giving them to yourself instead of openly expressing them and letting them out. Think about whether you really want to have that much anger or pain directed at yourself.

Use your dealings with people as a good opportunity to discover more about yourself.

## Rejection and Criticism

Well they hurt, don't they? But they also provide an excellent form of feedback. Unfortunately we tend to take them personally and act in a defensive manner, especially if they are about our wonderful craft: the good ship *Enterprise*.

Learning how to handle rejection is a must. If you're going to crawl away and hide for a year and a day when someone says no, both your business and your sense of self will suffer. It helps to remember that it is only actions which prompt rejections and criticisms, so when you next receive one, remember that it is aimed at the *actions* you performed, not at you personally.

As with conflicts, both criticisms and rejections offer opportunities for learning about either your product, your service or yourself. If prospective clients criticize your product, concentrate on what they are saying and try to see whether they have some justification for pointing out any flaws or weaknesses. For example, by listening to what they have to say about the choice of colours you offer, you may find that others have mentioned this in the past, providing you with a good opportunity to make a change and possibly increase sales. If as the result of a buyer's criticism 50 per cent more people buy your widgets now they are black instead of blue, then let's have more criticisms!

If a proposal is rejected after having made what you believed to be a stunning presentation, get some feedback. It may be that the clients found your presentation too glitzy and not in keeping with the sobriety of their firm, or they may have found it difficult to hear your quiet public speaking voice so that half your important points failed to get across.

Criticism and rejection can feel like the end of the world, yet with practice you can learn to turn them around and find within them useful feedback for helping you move forward more quickly on both a professional and personal level.

## ▪ BOUNDARIES

Personal boundaries can work for us or against us. And when you're working at home, the boundary issues can be very important. Knowing where your own lie is vital if peace and harmony are to be maintained, for without this knowledge it becomes impossible to let others know clearly where they can and cannot go; what is acceptable to you and what isn't; and what your own cut-off points are.

When boundaries are too rigid they create problems for other people, making you appear inflexible and selfish. They create problems for you when they are too unclear or largely non-existent, enabling people to take advantage of you and your time. Frustrations can creep in when one day it's OK to interrupt and the next you meet any distraction with a verbal tirade. The ideal is to have firm but flexible boundaries which are stated clearly yet which can be negotiated as occasions demand, without you feeling as though you are compromising yourself or jeopardizing your position.

So, in order for you to be able to establish with others what is and is not acceptable, you need to be clear within your own mind about where your boundaries lie. Present or past conflicts might provide clues to where clarification is needed.

## ▪ FEARS

Will I fail? What will I do if I succeed? What if the customer doesn't like the order? What if I miss the deadline? When you're working for yourself there appear to be fears aplenty, yet all they do is hold you back. It's a shame they're not marketable or else you could probably set up a nice little sideline in them.

The only way in which to conquer fears is to face up to them squarely. They are your own internal bullies, leaving you quaking in the corner. As with any bully, once you face up to them they leave you alone.

Fears can take many forms, and you're particularly prone in the early days when you haven't yet gained the experience to know that everything works out all right in the end. For some the fear of success can be as real as the fear of failure is for others. And sometimes fears come in different disguises to try to trick us. For example, a fear of success might manifest itself in missed appointments or ill-health before a crucial meeting which would have been the one to take you into the big time.

Awareness is needed to enable you to identify your own fears, to analyse them and find out what they are telling you, although for deep-seated ones it may take another's professional helping hand to assist you in working through them.

## ▪ MEETING CHALLENGES

One thing you can be certain of when you become self-employed: you will be meeting plenty of challenges. Learning to welcome them can be difficult at first but, as they say, challenges are opportunities for growth – both personally and professionally. Meeting them may provide you with some unexpected bounties. Hal has found that they have provided him with a greater sense of real security: 'I feel more secure within myself because now I know I can look after myself. Before, someone else did – he was called the employer.'

Meeting each successive challenge and knowing you will come through gives a real boost to your confidence. Even if something appears to be a failure in someone else's eyes, you have at least come through and will know better how to handle it next time. You will be learning from it and growing. In turn your self-esteem will improve and as you grow so will your personality as you become a more rounded person, discovering more about yourself and your capabilities.

Challenges can provide you with a new sense of perspective on life. If you have come through one, then where will the next take you? Suddenly new doors start to open.

Work is a wonderful place in which to find out about yourself. And as you gradually start to remove the blocks and negative emotions which may have been holding you back you may find you can tap into undiscovered reserves of energy, come up with fantastic ideas which you might never have thought of before, and otherwise start to push back the boundaries of your personal limitations even further. Learning about yourself is the greatest and best challenge of all.

Here are mini-biographies of the homeworkers I interviewed at length and whose experiences have contributed significantly to the text:

**Alice** makes hand-made gifts and craft items. She made the move to self-employment and working from home in 1989 after a period of being unemployed. She lives in London.

**Barry** has worked as a writer and publisher from home since around 1970 – a confirmed homeworker! He lives in Middlesex.

**Carol** has been a freelance journalist since 1990. As work has expanded so has her need for extra space, and she is now planning to move from her studio flat in West London to something larger.

**Charles** left his teaching job mid-career and set up a language service with his Hungarian wife, operating from their London home.

**David** established his own complementary therapy practice at his home in Somerset in 1984 after a lengthy 'apprenticeship'.

**Derek** is an independent financial advisor and has worked from home since 1990.

**Gerald** has been working from home as a management consultant since he retired from his accountancy job with British Telecom in 1991.

**Gilly** worked in education until the call to self-employment came after a trip abroad gave her the idea of importing and wholesaling artefacts. Initially working part-time in partnership with a friend, Gilly now runs her own show from her home in Surrey.

**Hal** took voluntary redundancy from his middle-management job in an education authority. After odd-jobbing for a while he has established himself successfully as a freelance researcher.

**Hilary** worked for two years as a self-employed freelance trainer working from home, then spent some time as director of a training company, and has recently returned to self-employment and homeworking.

**Lara** has worked from home on and off and in various capacities (some employed, some self-employed) since 1984. Disability through ill-health eventually led her to establish a grave-tending business.

**Liz** decided to 'go it alone' in 1990, leaving her job in publishing to become a freelance graphic designer.

**Richard**, like Gerald, turned to self-employment after retirement – in his case after a career in the Civil Service.

**Simon** began working from home 11 years ago as a management consultant and freelance trainer.

**William** has worked from home as a radio/audio producer since 1980 – practically all his working life. While he does have to spend some time in the studio when each project reaches recording stage, all the other work involved he does from home.

## ▪ Appendix B
## Useful Addresses

## Home Business Organizations

### Own Base
Enquiries Department
68 First Avenue
Bush Hill Park
Enfield EN1 1BN
*A networking organization for people who work from home (send SAE for details)*

### Telecottage Association
0800 616008

## Enterprise Information

### British Coal Enterprise Ltd
Hobart House
40 Grosvenor Place
London SW1X 7AE
0171–630 5304
*Assists businesses wishing to set up in former coal-mining areas*

### British Steel (Industry) Ltd
Canterbury House

2–6 Sydenham Road
Croydon CR9 2LJ
0181–686 2311
*Assists businesses wishing to set up in former steel-working areas*

### Business Links
0114 259 7507
*For details of your local One-Stop Shop offering information about all enterprise and business support in your area*

### European Information Line
0117 944 4888
*For information about conducting business in Europe*

### Livewire
Hawthorne House
Forth Banks
Newcastle-upon-Tyne NE1 3SG
0191–261 5584
*Help and advice for young entrepreneurs*

**Local Enterprise Development Unit**
LEDU House
Upper Galwally
Belfast BT8 4TB
01232 491031

**Prince's Youth Business Trust**
5th Floor
5 Cleveland Place
London SW1Y 6JJ
0171–321 6500
*Help and advice for young entrepreneurs*

**Rural Development Commission**
11 Cowley Street
London SW1P 3NB
0171–276 6969

## Business Support

**Association of British Chambers of Commerce**
9 Tufton Street
London SW1P 3QB
0171–222 1555

**Breakthrough Club**
Breakthrough Centre
7 Poplar Mews
Uxbridge Road
London W12 7JS
0181–749 8525

**Support for Partners of Entrepreneurs**
Gloucestershire TEC: 01452 524488
*A new initiative initially operating in the Gloucestershire area but hoping to develop nationwide*

**Business in the Community**
0171–629 1600

**Business Links**
0114 259 7507
*For details of your local One-Stop Shop offering information about all enterprise and business support in your area*

**Business Debtline**
Birmingham Settlement
318 Summer Lane
Newtown
Birmingham B19 3RL
0121–236 0595

**Federation of Small Businesses**
32 Orchard Road
Lytham St Annes
Lancs FY8 1NY
01253 720911

**Office of Fair Trading**
Field House
15–25 Bream's Buildings
London EC4A 1PR
0171–242 2858

## Professional Help

**Institute of Chartered Accountants**
Chartered Accountants' Hall
Moorgate Place
London EC2 2BJ
0171–920 8100
*For general enquiries and lists of chartered accountants in your area*

**Hospital Savings Association**
Hambledon House
Andover
Hants SP10 1BR
01264 353211

**Law Society**
113 Chancery Lane
London WC2A 1PL
0171–242 1222
*For general enquiries and lists of legal professionals in your area*

**Lawyers for Your Business**
0171–405 9075
*For lists of lawyers in this scheme which offers a free advisory interview for people setting up or running their own business*

## Disability

**Royal Association for Disability and Rehabilitation**
250 City Road
London EC1V 8AS
0171–250 3222
Minicom 0171–250 4119

## Child Care

**Parents at Work**
77 Holloway Road
London N7 8JZ
0171–700 5771

**Pre-School Playgroups Association**
61–63 King's Cross Road
London WC1X 9LL
0171–833 0991

**Professional Association of Nursery Nurses**
2 St James Court
Friar Gate
Derby DE1 1BT
01332 343029

## Health

**Association of Chartered Physiotherapists in Occupational Health**
14 Bedford Row
London WC1R 4ED
0171–242 1941

**Ergonomics Society**
Devonshire House
Devonshire Square
Loughborough
Leics LE11 3DW
01509 234904

**Health and Safety Executive**
Information Centre
Broad Lane
Sheffield S3 7HQ
0114 289 2345
Free leaflets line: 0114 289 2346

**Neville Johnson Fitted Furniture**
Broadoak Business Park
Ashburton Road West
Trafford Park
Manchester M17 1RW
0161 873 8333
*Suppliers of custom-made office furniture*

**RSI Association**
Chapel House
152 High Street
Yiewsley
West Drayton
Middx UB7 7BE
01895 431134

**Spectra Lighting**
York House
Lower Harlestone
Northampton NN7 4EW
01604 821904
*Suppliers of full-spectrum lighting*

## Counselling

**British Association for Counselling**
1 Regent Place
Rugby
Warwicks CV21 2PJ
01788 578328

**Co-counselling International**
c/o Westerly
Prestwick Lane
Chiddingford
Surrey GU8 4XW
*Send SAE with enquiry*

**Relate Marriage Guidance**
Herbert Gray College
Little Church Street
Rugby
Warwicks CV21 3AP
01788 573241

## Volunteering

**Volunteer Centre UK**
Carriage Row
183 Eversholt Street
London NW1 1BU
0171–388 9888
*For information on volunteering opportunities in your area*

## Information

**National Association for Citizens Advice Bureaux**
Middleton House
115–123 Pentonville Road
London N1 9LZ
0171–833 2181

# ■ Appendix C
## Further Reading

### Home Business

Dianne Baker, *Running a Home-Based Business* (Kogan Page, 1994)

Andrew Bibby, *Home Is Where the Office Is: A Practical Handbook for Teleworking from Home* (Headway, 1991)

British Telecom, *A Guide to Working from Home* (free from BT: 0800 800878)

Graham Jones, *How to Start a Business from Home* (How to Books, 2nd ed, 1991)

Ian Phillipson, *How to Work from Home* (How to Books, 1992)

Sue Read, *The Complete Guide to Working from Home* (Headline, 1992)

John Viney and Stephanie Jones, *One Man Band* (Thorsons, 1992)

### Personal Management

Jacqueline Atkinson, *Better Time Management* (Thorsons, 1992)

Peter Chatterton, *Technology Tools for Your Home Business* (Kogan Page, 1992)

Dr Windy Dryden, *Beating the Comfort Trap* (Sheldon Press, 1993)

Diane Fassel, *Working Ourselves to Death* (Thorsons, 1992)

Marek Gitlin, *Making Time Work For You*, (Sheldon Press, 1990)

Christine Ingham, *Life Without Work* (Thorsons, 1994)

Ray Josephs, *How to Gain an Extra Hour Every Day* (Thorsons, 1994)

Gerard Morfett and Geraldine Brown, *Making Time* (BBC Books, 1993)

John Mulligan, *Personal Management Handbook* (Sphere, 1988)

Susan Perry and Jim Dawson, *Be At Your Best When It Really Counts* (Thorsons, 1990)

Odette Pollar, *Get Organised!* (Kogan Page, 1993)

*Reader's Digest Household Hints and Handy Tips* (Reader's Digest Books, 1992)

Mike Woods and Jackie Whitehead (in association with Diana Lamplugh),

*Working Alone: Surviving and Thriving* (Institute of Management; Pitman Publishing, 1993)

## Health

Jonathan Drake, *Thorsons Introductory Guide to the Alexander Technique* (Thorsons, 1993)

Susannah and Leslie Kenton, *Endless Energy* (Vermilion, 1993)

Dr Carl Pfeiffer, *Nutrition and Mental Health* (Thorsons, 1991)

## Using Professional Help

Consumers Association, *Making the Most of Professional Services* (Consumers Association and Hodder and Stoughton, 1989)

Geoffrey Smith, *Getting the Best from Agencies & Other Outside Services* [re: Marketing] (Kogan Page, 1994)

## Self-Development

Jack Black, *MindStore* (Thorsons, 1994)

Erika J. Chopich and Margaret Paul, *Healing Your Aloneness* (Thorsons, 1990)

Richard Denny, *Motivate to Win* (Kogan Page, 1993)

Jinny Ditzler, *Your Best Year Yet!* (Thorsons, 1994)

Dr Paul Hauck, *How to Be Your Own Best Friend* (Sheldon Press, 1988)

Susan Jeffers, *Feel the Fear and Do It Anyway* (Century Hutchinson, 1987)

Janette Rainwater, *Self-Therapy: A Guide to Becoming Your Own Therapist* (Aquarian Press, 1989)

Dru Scott, *Stress that Motivates* (Kogan Page, 1993)

Robert Sharpe, *Assert Yourself: How to Do a Good Deal Better With Others* (Kogan Page, 1989)

## Self-Help

Judy Wilson, *Self-Help Groups: Getting Started; Keeping Going* (Longmans, 1986)

## Relationships

Sarah Litvinoff, *The Relate Guide to Better Relationships* (Vermilion, 1992)

## Magazines

*Enterprise Magazine*
(Entrepreneur Magazines
Ltd, Haland House, 66 York
Road, Weybridge, Surrey,
KT13 9DY; 01932 829920).
Monthly

*Home Business* (Merlin
Publications Ltd, 14 Hove
Business Centre, Fonthill
Road, Hove, BN3 6HA;
01273 888994). Monthly

*Home Run* (79 Black Lion
Lane, London, W6 9BG;
0181–846 9244).
Subscription only

*Teleworker* (Magazine of the
Telecottage Association,
Wren Telecottage, Stoneleigh
Park, Warwicks CV8 2RR;
01203 696986.)

# ■ Index